IMAGES
of America

BETHLEHEM

IMAGES
of America

BETHLEHEM

Bethlehem Area Public Library
Edited by Kathleen Stewart

ARCADIA
PUBLISHING

Copyright © 1997 by Bethlehem Area Public Library
ISBN 978-1-5316-2217-6

Published by Arcadia Publishing
Charleston, South Carolina

Library of Congress Catalog Card Number: 2004115249

For all general information contact Arcadia Publishing at:
Telephone 843-853-2070
Fax 843-853-0044
E-mail sales@arcadiapublishing.com
For customer service and orders:
Toll-Free 1-888-313-2665

Visit us on the Internet at www.arcadiapublishing.com

Contents

A Bethlehem Family Photo Album: 1845–1990

An exhibit of 350 photographs, selected from over 600 photos submitted by community residents, displayed in the windows of the Bethlehem Area Public Library from June 1, 1991 — July 4, 1992.

Presented by the Photography Committee
of the 250th Anniversary Cultural Committee

Tim Gilman, Chairman
Gerald R. Bastoni, Curator
Dr. Frederick G. Gilmartin, Concept
Dr. Paul Larson, Consulting Humanist, PHC Grant
Marlene Gilley, Cultural Committee Chairman
Thomas Cunningham
Robert Cunningham
Nevin Yeakel

The exhibit designed and produced by:
Rileigh, Gander & Showalter, Inc.,
Lehigh Valley Photographic Services, Inc.

The Bethlehem Area Public Library
would like to additionally thank

The Pharo Foundation

and

The Community Residents
who graciously gave us permission
to reproduce their photos in this book.

Preface

A Bethlehem Family Photo Album.

This was a different kind of history exhibit. This was a history exhibit that was by the people and for the people: the citizens of Bethlehem, Pennsylvania.

Almost all history exhibits originate from the collections of museums or individuals. They are assembled by professional curators and often reflect personal interests or points of view. They usually present photographs taken by professionals, artists, and serious amateurs whose interests also shape photographic images and their contents.

But this was a different kind of history exhibit. The photographs in this exhibit came from the family albums of the city's residents. Citizens working together to celebrate their community's 250th anniversary achieved a very personal and meaningful reconnection to the past. In categories that mirrored daily activity—work, leisure, family, neighborhood, worship, and education—they presented the stories of their lives and their transitions. The photographs were taken through the loving eyes of family and friends for personal enjoyment and reflection. They remind us of the special quality of ordinary moments and familiar places. For a family, such photographs are a direct personal and emotional connection to the past.

The most successful history exhibits are those that change the ways people look at the past. The power of history is released through the process of active remembering and personal involvement. The citizens of Bethlehem, Pennsylvania, created an act of community remembering that was both highly personal and universally human.

This was definitely a different kind of history exhibit.

Jerry Bastoni
Bethlehem, Pennsylvania
February 1997

Introduction

Bethlehem is a reinterpretation of the photograph exhibit that was presented in celebration of the community's 250th anniversary. Much effort was made to make sure that photographs from as many donors as possible were utilized. Unfortunately, it was not feasible to include every photograph that was released for publication in this work. Often, photographs that looked wonderful exhibited in the windows of the library would have lost much of their power when reduced to fit the pages of this book. Omissions were, therefore, made in the best interest of the work.

Occasionally, the captions that originally accompanied the photographs were changed. Modifications were either the result of additional research or were made to accommodate the space limitations of the layout. Intense copyediting hopefully insured the proper spelling of all names and locations. Any errors were, of course, not intentional, but were probably the result of intense eye-strain.

Comprehensive histories of Bethlehem have been written, and I am certain many more will be. While connections and common threads are noticeable throughout this work, each photograph tells its own story. Therefore, the material that makes up the bulk of the captions is not necessarily intended to teach the reader anything, but to bring the photographs to life and deliver the reader back in time. There is no reason to believe that I could have expressed the circumstances and sentiments of the photographs any better than the Bethlehemites who actually lived when they were taken; therefore, language contemporary to the pictures was used where possible.

I would like to extend my thanks to Jack M. Berk, Executive Director of the Bethlehem Area Public Library, for offering me the opportunity to put this book together. I am especially indebted to Jane Gill, Public Services Division Coordinator at the library, whose creativity and knowledge greatly enhanced this work.

Hopefully, *Bethlehem*, the product of a non-Bethlehemite, will prove to be to the satisfaction of the community that made it possible.

K. Stewart
Bethlehem, Pennsylvania
March 1997

One

Cityscape

Eighteenth-century industrial area, now Historic Bethlehem, circa 1880. (Robert Cunningham.) The Moravians, who founded Bethlehem in 1741, established a fairly extensive industrial area along the Monocacy Creek. A gristmill, butchery, smithy, and a candlemaker's shop were just a few of the businesses that made the community largely self-sufficient. The Luckenbach Grist Mill is in the rear to the left. The stone buildings in front of the mill are the Dye House and an attached dwelling. The Tannery, to the right, continued to process hides into leather until the 1860s. Historic Bethlehem Incorporated restored the Tannery, and it was opened to the public in 1971.

Luckenbach Mill, north facade, 1900. (Historic Bethlehem Incorporated.) "The milliners smelled the smoke, and made diligent search for its cause throughout the entire building but, not finding it, went to bed, supposing something might be burning in the neighborhood." After several hours of smoldering, the grain that had fallen in to the hot flue burst into an ungovernable fire, destroying Luckenbach Mill on the evening of January 27, 1869. Though *The Bethlehem Daily Times* reported that there "were a few fools . . . who did nothing but jabber and yell," the hardy and dedicated firemen kept the blaze from spreading to other buildings and from claiming any lives. Following the fire, the Luckenbach brothers built the larger brick structure pictured above.

Looking northeast across the Lehigh Canal to Bethlehem, 1900. (Earl L. Anders.) What was once a bustling district of West Bethlehem is now a largely grassy area that serves as home to the Celtic Classic and Musikfest's Kunstplatz. The Central Railroad of New Jersey station, now the Main Street Depot Restaurant, is seen to the far right of the shot. The larger white building toward the middle of the photograph was Fetters Hotel, located at 10 S. Main Street. At this time, Lehigh Avenue (now Lehigh Street) ran from the limits of the borough on the west eastward to the Monocacy Creek and was largely residential.

Sun Hotel on Main Street, circa 1870. (Robert and Thomas Cunningham.) The Sun Hotel, built in the late 1750s, was operated by the Bethlehem Moravian congregation until 1830. At the time of this photograph, it was owned by Charles Brodhead, who purchased the Sun in 1868 for $50,000. The hotel maintained a reputation as a place of comfort and quality well into the late nineteenth century. An advertisement in 1881 declared, "The Sun is handsomely furnished throughout, and in its equipment and management will have no superior place."

Sun Hotel omnibus on Main Street, 1868. (Robert and Thomas Cunningham.) Guests at the Sun Hotel were met at the rail station by an omnibus from the hotel's own livery and then delivered directly to the inn. In 1881, the livery was enhanced by the latest in four-wheeled transportation. *The Bethlehem Daily Times* reported that "Kirschner, the Sun Hotel Liveryman, has just received from New York a vehicle known as a landau, the first of its kind in Bethlehem. It is comfortable and stylish, and just the thing for pleasure riding, either in pleasant or inclement weather. It is for hire."

11

Civil War statue at top of Market Street Hill, 1904. (Bob Carlen.) Politics were no small affair in Bethlehem in 1904. In celebration of Theodore Roosevelt's victory over Alton B. Parker, "shortly after midnight, when indications pointed to Republican success, the Lincoln Republican Association formed a procession on Market Street." Appropriately, the group had hung its banner from the city's monument dedicated to "those who gave their lives to the Union." Erected in 1887 by the J.K. Taylor Post #182 of the Grand Army Republic, the monument became a road hazard in the twentieth century, receiving many scars from Market Street motorists on foggy nights. It was moved to the Bethlehem Rose Garden in late 1967.

Looking south on Main Street from corner of Market Street, 1905. (Mrs. William B. Leckonby.) Charles David Bishop was the first landlord for the Eagle (located on the right), which opened in December 1823. The hotel provided lodging for the parents of many young women attending the Seminary down the street, as well as "numerous gentlemen and ladies of the cities of Philadelphia, New York, and Baltimore . . . who annually resort to Bethlehem . . . to enjoy a healthy country air." In 1919, the Eagle was destroyed in preparation for the construction of the Hotel Bethlehem.

Main Street looking south, 1919. (John G. Kichline.) If getting down Main Street, especially during Musikfest and the busy Christmas season, is tough today, imagine the chaos that ensued in 1919. Shoppers and merchants trying to get to their places of business had to fight different modes of transportation, including the horse and carriage, motorcar, and trolley, all vying for right-of-way on a crowded and busy street. Apparently, though, the Bethlehem police, who "studied the traffic question very carefully," found pedestrians to be the major problem and declared that conditions "would be greatly improved and chances of accidents decreased if pedestrians would cross at street intersections only."

Looking north on Main Street from Church Street, 1921. (Emerson J. and Arlene S. Mills.) In 1921, conspicuous on Main Street's skyline was the construction of the Hotel Bethlehem, seen just behind the trees. Started in June of that year, the hotel was ready for business by May 1922. An advertisement in the *Globe* invited the public "to inspect this beautiful and modern hostelry, erected on the site of the Old Eagle Hotel . . . at a cost of over One Million Dollars. The facilities of this up-to-date place of public entertainment and service are equal to those offered by any hotel in the State."

13

Outside City Market, Third Street, South Bethlehem, 1920. (Anthony J. Rich.) Every Tuesday, Thursday, and Saturday morning, the South Side Market would bustle with activity as city residents bartered with hucksters from out of town over fresh produce and meat. In 1920, butter could be purchased for 75¢ a pound, oysters for $1.50 per hundred, peaches for 25¢ a quarter peck, and potatoes for $1.25 a bushel. Poultry could be had for 42¢ a pound live weight or 72¢ a pound dressed.

Broad and Main Streets, 1938. (Melvin W. Hoch.) At 8 pm, Friday, December 2, 1938, Mrs. Eugene Grace threw the switch that illuminated Bethlehem for another Christmas season. The Hill-to-Hill Bridge, Main Street, Third Street, Broad Street, and other avenues simultaneously began to glow, as the city's "still essentially religious" celebration of the Savior's birth began. *The Bethlehem Globe Times* commented, "Quick to follow fickle fashion's dictates, the decorations now boast of neon stars gleaming along Main, Broad, and Third Streets instead of last year's cello-glass twinklers."

Looking south down Main Street, 1939. (Dennis M. Kery.) A constant stream of black sedans flowed in and out of Bethlehem's central shopping thoroughfare in 1939. In the days before shopping strips and shopping malls, families would take trips to town, each member finding something of interest. Perhaps the kids would browse through Woolworth's 5¢ to $1.00 store at 555 Main, while Mom had her hair done at the Queenie Beauty Shop down the street. Meantime, Dad would take a peek at Brown-Borhek Company's new building supplies and then pick up some Lucky Strikes at Keystone Cigarette Sales before rounding up the family and heading home.

The Old Homestead Fruit and Poultry Farm Stand, Joseph E. Seifert, 1930. (Paul J. Seifert.) Joseph E. Seifert filled his truck with apples, vegetables, eggs, and chickens every Saturday morning and headed for the City Market on Broad Street. In the afternoon, he went on a huckster route, selling more goods to people in the area. The Old Homestead Farm, where Joseph was born and raised, had been in the family since the eighteenth century. The family continued to operate the orchards into the 1950s, and then converted the farm to strictly dairy production in the 1960s. The farm was named a Bicentennial Farm in 1988 in conjunction with the 200th anniversary of the Constitution and was sold by the family in 1989.

15

Construction of Broad Street Bridge, looking east, 1909. (Nevin Yeakel.) The original Broad Street Bridge was built in 1871. A toll was added two years later to absorb the costs of repairs. By 1909, increased traffic and more modern materials led to its replacement by a wider and sturdier bridge. The roadway, which West Side contractor Joseph Craig and hundreds of workmen laid, contained 900 cubic feet of cinders, stones, old bricks, and dirt. The cement was manufactured just up the road in Stockertown by the Northampton Cement Company.

Hill-to-Hill Bridge construction at Main and Church Streets, 1922. (Nancy Labert.) For many years there had been talk of building a free bridge to span the Lehigh River between Bethlehem and South Bethlehem. Finally, in the early 1920s, enough men and money were gathered to make the bridge a reality. Above, workers along the Main Street branch of the bridge distribute cement through a system of chutes. Four hundred and twenty-five thousand bags of cement from the Pennsylvania Cement Company were dispersed into 107,000 cubic yards of concrete for the bridge.

16

"Break Time": Joe Jordan-(on left) and unknown carpenter, Hill-to-Hill Bridge construction, 1922. (Nancy Labert.) A campaign by the movers and shakers of early twentieth century Bethlehem raised just over $1 million for the construction of the Hill-to-Hill Bridge. Charles Schwab contributed $50,000 of the quarter million that individual contributors gave towards the project. His company, the Bethlehem Steel Corporation, threw in $200,000 for good measure, but ideas and money only go so far. Without men like Joe Jordan, left, and his pal, the dream held by the city's men of property and standing would never have become a physical reality. Hundreds of contractors, craftsmen, and unskilled laborers completed the bridge in just over three years.

Hill-to-Hill Bridge from South Mountain, 1925. (John G. Waidner.) Countless people and animals lost their lives to the dangers of the at-grade crossings of four different railroads. Many others were left maimed or crippled. The bridge was built largely to curb these senseless accidents. Eight entrance ramps, including one for pedestrians at Main Street, elevated all traffic above the rail crossings. On November 1, 1924, the day of the unofficial opening of the bridge, the editor of the *Globe* remarked, "It stretches out its arms to all parts of the city, over river, creek and canal and draws them together into one great community."

The old Broad Street Bridge over the Monocacy Creek, 1890. (Gertrude M. Helms.) Opening on May 1, 1871, the Broad Street Bridge "was crossed by thousands" for the first time. "A magnificent view can be had from the bridge, and on that account it will no doubt become a popular promenade," apparently, for human and animal alike. In August 1880, the *Bethlehem Daily Times* reported that a "large flock of sheep and lambs crossed Broad Street Bridge. They were in [the] charge of several drovers. Starting from Crawford County five weeks ago, they were accompanied by a large camp wagon, a big watch dog, a goat, a cow and a young colt."

18

Union Depot, South Bethlehem, 1900. (Carl J. Spangenberg.) On November 18, 1867, "four big gray horses, decked with the stars and stripes" drew a coach carrying local dignitaries to the new Union Depot in South Bethlehem. Jointly used by the Lehigh Valley Railroad and the North Penn., the new station was "as much an honor to Bethlehem and the railroad companies as the old one was a disgrace to both." In 1924, this structure was replaced by a more modern passenger station that continued to service both railroads.

Bethlehem Airport, east end of South Mountain, circa 1930. (Sandra P. McKinney.) Located at the Hellertown-Bethlehem border, the Bethlehem Municipal Airport was dedicated in October 1929. Not a passenger terminal, the airport specialized in flight instruction, air shows, and sightseeing tours. It also served as the home base of Jim Ryan's aerial photography company and was once visited by Amelia Earhart. Located on Steel-owned land leased by the city, it operated from 1929 to 1934. In 1934, the city purchased the land, closed the airport, and used the hangar as a storehouse until 1941, when they sold it back to the company.

End of East Broad trolley and call box, near Pfeifle Field, 1941. (Dennis M. Kery.) The Philadelphia Division of the Lehigh Valley Transit Company (LVTC) advertised travel between Philadelphia and the Lehigh Valley as the Liberty Bell Route, in honor of the soldiers who fled British-occupied Philadelphia in 1777 with the famous bell. The LVTC purchased car #55 from the Indiana Railroad Company in February 1941 and converted it into car #1030. They adjusted the exterior, but the club car interior furnishings, including upholstered chairs and sofas, a carpeted floor, lavatory facilities, and potted plants, remained. On September 7, 1951, the last rail car completed the Liberty Bell Route because the LVTC converted its electric rail service to an auto-bus service.

Clearing snow at Taylor Field, Lehigh University, pre-1915. (Ruth Hemmerly Kelly.) Between 1897–1909, sports at Lehigh were nothing to brag about. Then, largely with money and resources donated by alumni, winning coaches and quality athletes were wooed to the South Side, and facilities were built to match their talents. Taylor Field, pictured above, was expanded and improved in 1914 and was renamed Taylor Stadium. On November 21, 1987, with windchills well below zero, the Engineers handed the Lafayette Leopards a 17-10 loss in the final game ever played at Taylor Stadium.

Family outing on South Mountain, Imre Kukor and Joseph Slavics families, 1921. (Mary Leiderman.) Though not a company town per se, the sights, sounds, and smells from the steel mills constantly reminded workers and their families who lived on the South Side of Bethlehem where their livelihoods came from. Their homes, naturally, were located close to the works for reasons of convenience and economy. Even Sunday escapes to nature often took place in the shadows of the mills, as the cost of trolley rides out to the park lands were often prohibitive for laborers and their large families and were reserved only for special occasions.

View of the Heights, 1950. (Andrew Lisowski.) In 1950, Eugene Grace boasted to the Chamber of Commerce that the Steel employed twenty thousand people in Bethlehem alone, with a payroll of over $6 million a month and an annual capacity of 15,000,000 tons corporation-wide. In 1967, though, the Heights, a residential district near the Steel, fell victim to redevelopment and company expansion. Storms of protest by residents brought "charges of a sinister plot, of discrimination, of disregard for the poor and of pressure tactics" used to remove the families. Two hundred and eight buildings, housing over two hundred families, were knocked down to make way for Bethlehem Steel's basic oxygen furnace complex, which has since been closed.

21

West Lincoln Street from Decatur Street, 1947. (Nathan Tumminello.) "The Housing Shortage in Bethlehem is one of the most serious and perplexing problems with which we have ever been confronted," declared Mayor Robert Pfeifle in January 1948. "It is most pathetic and it seriously affects the home-life of many families, and that is where our Democratic way of life begins." In an effort to alleviate the housing crisis, a Bethlehem Trailer Camp, with 120 units renting for between $18 and $22 each a month, was set up by the Federal Public Housing Authority for ex-GIs and their families. Construction also went along at a good clip, with over thirty-one new streets graded and opened in 1946 alone.

"Grandpa's Little Girl": Robert and Carol Wesner, Kaywin Avenue, 1951. (Carol Wesner Lutz.) One of the ways in which Bethlehem dealt with the post-war housing shortage was with the construction of suburban housing, specifically with what the *Bethlehem Globe* called the "Lehigh Valley's boomingest bedroom—the city's new Northwest Section." Little Carol Wesner's neighborhood on Kaywin Avenue was considered, in 1957, to be "the granddaddy and still the largest of them all." Between 1951 and 1957, almost five hundred ranches, split-levels, two-stories, and doubles homes had been built.

"First Bike": Dale Wesner, 1454 Kaywin Avenue, 1954. (Mrs. Ken Wesner.) Dale Wesner surely had little trouble finding friends to go bike riding with in his Northwest neighborhood. Reported to be "the friendliest in the world," the families who moved to Kaywin Avenue and the surrounding area typically consisted of a former GI, his wife, and their two children. The father, more than likely, worked at Bethlehem Steel or Western Electric. A good job and the GI Bill enabled him to put $600 down on a $14,000 split-level and pay $53 a month on a 30-year mortgage. Dale's dad, a draftsman at the Steel, fit this criteria well.

Flood of the Lehigh River, Lehigh Street Ramp, 1955. (William Poczak.) Thanks to Hurricane Diane, the Lehigh River at Bethlehem crested at 22.67 feet between August 18–19, 1955. The residents of the Riverside Hotel, seen to the left of the photograph, were evacuated due to the rising waters; a Bethlehem Steel shut-down idled 20,000 workers; the sewage disposal plant went out of operation; and early morning commuters in Bethlehem parked their cars on the streets and left buses in order to make their treks to work on foot. All in all, damage was estimated at more than $10 million.

23

Construction of Route 378, Ken and Diane Beaver in pipes, 1966. (Ken Beaver.) Burgeoning new suburbs and increased traffic to Bethlehem made the construction of a highway from the Lehigh Valley Thruway to the Hill-to-Hill Bridge not only desirable, but necessary. Groundbreaking ceremonies for the $12-million roadway took place in March 1966, and the route was opened almost exactly one year later. The children of nearby neighborhoods found the construction site almost too much to resist. The *Bethlehem Globe Times* reported in June 1967 that the "workers were not able to control the children," who were riding bikes through the site and playing in newly poured concrete.

Ground breaking for new city center, East Church Street, 1965. (Betty M. Risk.) On May 19, 1965, under a hot and sunny sky, the ground was broken for Bethlehem's new city center at 10 East Church Street. From left to right in the photograph are: Robert L. Dutt, of the Junior Chamber of Commerce; Gary Dologite, a Liberty High School student; police officer Jackson Strohl; Edward Hudak, a first grade student from Ss. Cyril and Methodius School; A.C. Snyder, president of the Bethlehem Senior Citizen Council; fireman Walker Daniels; and the mayor of Bethlehem, H. Gordon Payrow. The Liberty High School band, Miss Lehigh Valley, a Marine color guard, and over 650 spectators were also on hand to celebrate this major event.

Two

Service

Baby Health Station, East Second Street, South Bethlehem, 1918. (Bob Carlen.) These two young mothers and their children probably lived longer, healthier lives thanks to Dr. C.F. Welden (on left), Superintendent Rachel Mifflin (middle), and Assistant Nurse Elizabeth Wheat, all of the city's Baby Health Station. Progressive Mayor Archibald Johnston wrote of the station, organized in 1915, "it is hoped to give every young American citizen a fair start in health toward up-standing manhood and womanhood . . . as well as conserving the vigor and time and ease of mind of parents for industrial efficiency and the general economic good."

St. Luke's Hospital, 1888. (Melba Weaver.) St. Luke's Hospital was established to fill the needs of an increasingly industrial area. Injured workers from the industrial concerns of Catasauqua, Hokendauqua, and Allentown, and also from Bethlehem's two major industries, the Bethlehem Iron Company and the New Jersey Zinc and Iron Co., no longer had to endure long, often painful trips to Philadelphia hospitals. Originally located at 325 Broadway, the hospital was moved in 1876 to the "Water Cure" property of German homeopathic doctor Frances H. Oppert.

St. Luke's Hospital ambulances, circa 1929. (Robert F. Szakos.) Driver Joseph Szakos Sr. sits behind the wheel of St. Luke's first motor ambulance, which the hospital acquired in 1919. To the left is the hospital's new 1929 model ambulance. Without a doubt, the ambulances became increasingly important as the city's population grew. Industrial accidents were common, precipitated by long work-weeks and the occasional twenty-four hour swing shift, making exhausted workers vulnerable to hot, heavy, and dangerous equipment in the mills.

First Capping Ceremony, candy stripers, St. Luke's Hospital, 1960. (Ellie O'Donnell.) High school friends Pat Mezza and Ellie Horvath became candy stripers together for St. Luke's Hospital. Trained to work with patients, the girls spent two years writing letters, filling water glasses, delivering flowers, and just keeping company with patients on the wards. Pat and Ellie were among the first six candy stripers to receive their white caps, a sign of dedication and knowledge proven by many hours of service. Pictured above, from left to right, are: (front row) Kathy Rehm, Janet Phillips, and Carol Yetter; (back row) Pat Mezza, Genevieve Weber, and Ellie Horvath.

First Board of Directors, YWCA., 1929. (Kathleen Widner/Carolyn S. Emrich.) Associational life for the young women of Bethlehem existed in several different forms since the nineteenth century. The Bethlehem Girls Club, organized in 1917, expanded into the YWCA in 1927, at which time the group boasted more than 1,300 charter members. A clipping from 1943 touted the YWCA as "a great adventure in democracy. It is a cross section of people . . . an organization which makes no distinction in race, creed or color and fills the intellectual and civic needs of women and girls in all walks of life."

27

Red Cross volunteers, Rhoda Edwards (on left) and Christine Sayre, 1917. (Elizabeth T. Diamond.) The Bethlehem chapter of the American Red Cross was organized on June 27, 1917. Women from all across the city contributed to the war effort by sewing bandages for the soldiers in Europe. Additionally, the young women helped run a Red Cross canteen located at the Union Depot, "dispensing cheer and refreshments to soldiers and sailors." On Tuesday, October 15, 1918, these young women greeted more than one hundred soldiers passing through Bethlehem with cigarettes, chocolate, and magazines, for which they were "particularly grateful."

Pioneer Young Colored Women, first black women graduates of Red Cross Home Hygiene and Care of the Sick course, 1940. (Cordelia E. Miller.) Thelma Francis Jenkins (center, back row) wanted very much to become a registered nurse, but no programs in the Lehigh Valley were open to "colored" women at the time. She heard of a practical nursing course being offered in town, but she needed to complete the American Red Cross (ARC) home nursing course before entering. She contacted ARC's Bethlehem Chapter, which had never been confronted with a "colored" woman desiring to take the course. After much consideration, they agreed to provide a segregated course for interested black women in the area. The twelve women enrolled would only pass, however, if all the women successfully completed the course. Needless to say, and much to the surprise of the nurse and doctor teaching the course, everyone passed with flying colors.

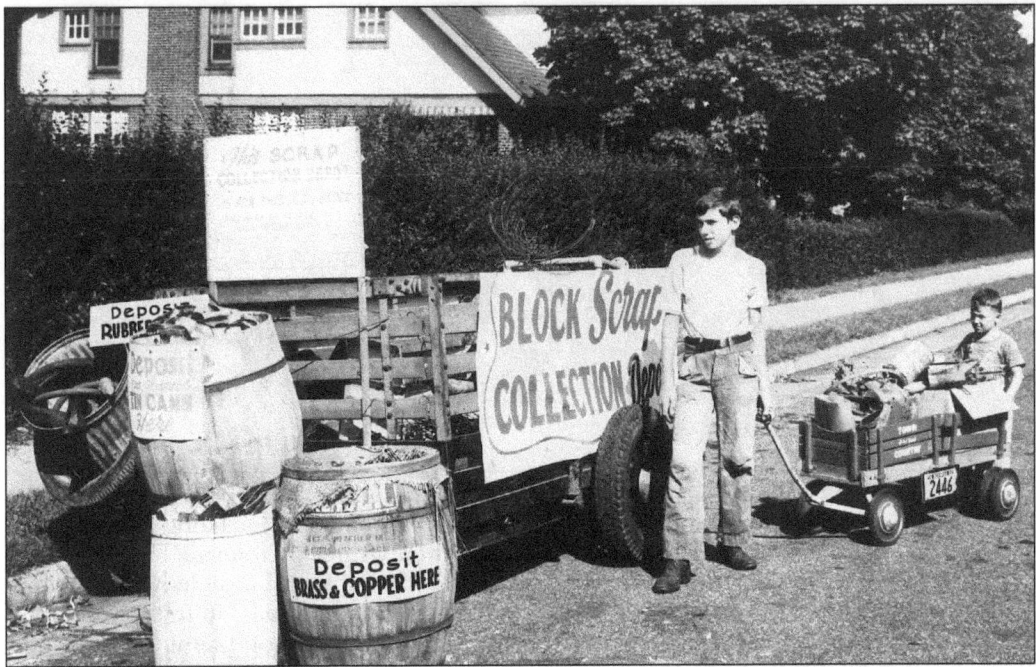

World War II scrap drive, 1944. (Bob Carlen.) Bethlehem citizens, young and old, heeded the call of the Office of Civilian Defense and Mayor Robert Pfeifle. From 1941 to the end of World War II, they made it their "patriotic duty" to collect scrapmetal, rubber, paper rags, and tin for the war effort. The mayor bragged that "to help win the battle of production, Bethlehem joined with the rest of the Nation in a continuing campaign to salvage every bit of material that could be used to help defeat the Axis and Japs."

First Bethlehem Police Motorcycle Force, East Fourth Street, 1917. (Mary K. Bishop.) Motorcycles made the jobs of Bethlehem's police officers easier in a city that was growing and modernizing quickly. The mayor endorsed the police as a benefit to the people of the city. "Contrary to the popular notion that the exercise by the city of its police powers tends to limit the freedom of action of the individual, it actually operates to *promote* liberty and the fullest enjoyment of one's personal rights, provided the police officers faithfully discharge their duties and give every inhabitant a *square deal.*"

City of Bethlehem Police Department in front of Liberty High School, 1923. (Neal Lamana.) In 1923, the police department employed fifty-one men in uniform, including four mounted and three motorcycle officers, one patrol driver, and twenty-three patrolmen. That year, they handled over 2,100 complaints, including arrests for 752 drunk and disorderly, 52 raids on bawdy houses, 1 adultery, and 1 murder. Eleven traffic officers handled 336 traffic violations, though the supervisor of police assured the citizenry that "with everyone turning to the right and looking in all directions as they approach street crossings, accidents will be reduced to a minimum." The next year, there were 420 violations.

Bethlehem Police Car #1, 1947. (Don Sabo.) Vincent D. Fresoli, above, had not been a member of the Bethlehem Police Department for long when this photograph was taken. A 1938 graduate of Liberty High School, Vincent joined the force in 1946. He was the first officer of the Juvenile Bureau in Bethlehem. For the last thirteen years of his career with the city, Officer Fresoli was the head of the Juvenile Bureau. He retired as a captain in 1966, the same year he married his wife Doris. Still a resident of Bethlehem, Vincent is a part-time Deputy Sheriff for Northampton County.

Traffic cop, Officer Arpad Kery, Main Street in front of Orr's, 1958. (Arpad Kery.) Arpad Kery joined the Bethlehem police force on July 16, 1949. A star football player for Liberty High School, he also served in the U.S. Navy. Officer Kery, who never missed a day's work, served over the years as head of the detective bureau, traffic captain, and president of the Middle Eastern Police Chiefs' Association. He retired from the force in 1975. Following his retirement, he was Lower Saucon's Chief of Police until January 1977.

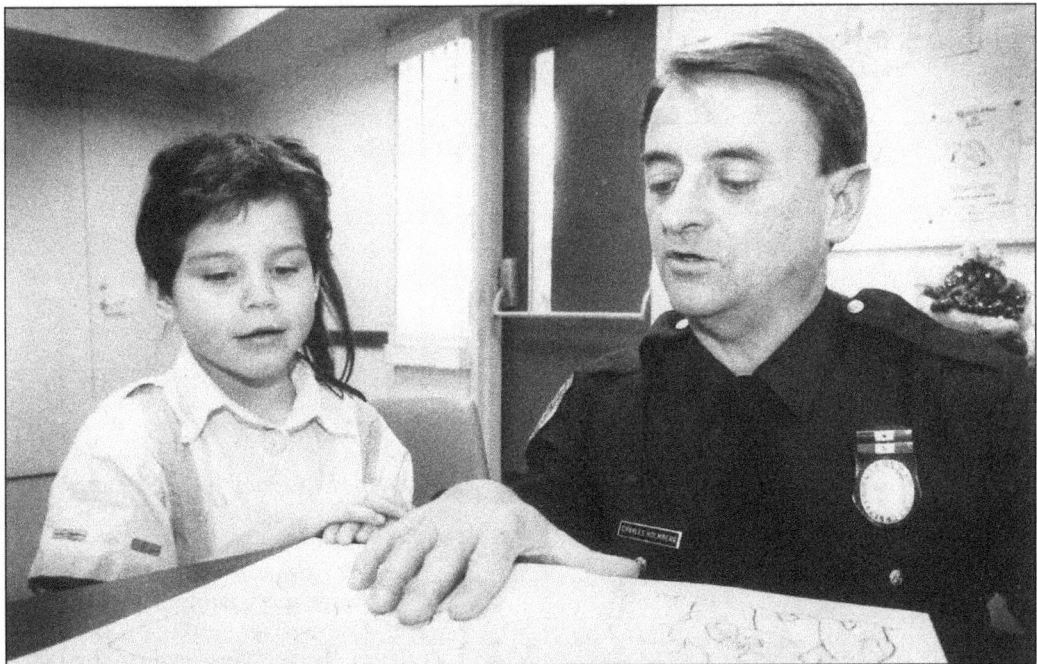

Officer Holmberg teaching drug prevention to Tamara Melendez, 1990. (Charles Holmberg.) After twenty-two years with the Bethlehem Police Department, Officer Charles Holmberg was named the city's drug education officer. Officer Holmberg graduated first among 36 officers attending a DARE (Drug Abuse Resistance Education) seminar in 1990. Through drug education in classrooms from kindergarten through fifth grade, Officer Holmberg presents police officers as positive role models for the community, helping children to build self-esteem and make lifestyle choices alternative to drugs and alcohol.

Fire equipment at Central High School, Vine Street, South Bethlehem, 1905. (Nancy Rutman.) The Liberty Fire Company, first organized as the Good Intent Hose in July 1874, was located at Vine and Fourth Streets and stood by the motto "We Labor for Public Good." At the annual banquet in 1905, former chief James A. Oldnam implored the firefighters, "No matter what time of day or night, in all kinds of weather, when the bell taps the number of the box, dress quick and turn out to help a friend or enemy alike, no distinction of creed or color, at the risk of life and limb, do all in your power to save life and property."

Reliance Engine House, 1912. (Barbara Fowler.) The Reliance Engine House, located at 24 East Broad Street, was equipped with "one Jones and Clapp steamer [and] one hose carriage carrying 800 feet of fabric hose." The company had fifty volunteer members who, upon returning from a fire, would hang the 800 feet of hose from the tower located behind the engine house. This was imperative, for if the hose was not thoroughly dried, it would rot and hinder their firefighting efforts.

Monocacy Fire Company Engine, Harry Grube, driver, 1910. (Carl J. Spangenberg.) The fire department of the city of Bethlehem consisted of five companies (Central Fire Station No. 1, Reliance Fire Co. No. 3, Fairview Hose Co. No. 4, Monocacy Hose Co. No. 1, and Lehigh Hose Co. No. 5), one chief, five assistant chiefs, three paid drivers, two steam engineers, three chemical engineers, two stokers, two pipemen, and one tillerman. The Monocacy Hose Co., for which Harry Grube was the driver, was originally incorporated as Fetter Hose Co. No. 1 and was located on Prospect Avenue. In 1910, the company had fifty-five volunteers and one fully equipped combination truck.

City of Bethlehem Firemen's Parade, Church Street, 1915. (Melody J. Raub.) The South Bethlehem Semi-Centennial came to an end on Saturday, October 9, 1915, after a full week of celebrations. The "climax of the pageants took place, Saturday afternoon, when the firemen had their day. The parade was beautiful and impressive, about 2,000 firemen of the state participating accompanied by fine bands and drum corps." Companies from Norristown, Quakertown, Towanda, Harrisburg, and Phillipsburg joined local firemen in the spectacle, and the Bethlehem men showed off "their new motor apparatus recently purchased . . . for the first time in the parade."

Boy Scout Troop 2, First Presbyterian Church (now Trinity UCC), Center and North Streets, 1928. (Edwin S. Erickson Jr.) In 1910, American businessman William D. Boyce was inspired by a British boy scout who guided him through the foggy streets of London. Upon returning to the states, he founded the Boy Scouts of America. Troop 2, the oldest Boy Scout troop in Bethlehem, is now known as Troop 302. Since 1917, the First Presbyterian church, has sponsored the scouts as part of their Outreach-to-Youth program. Without a doubt, these young men also lived to help other people at all times and to keep themselves "Physically Strong, Mentally Awake, and Morally Straight."

Girl Scout Troop presents play, Donegan School Troop, 1944. (Clara M. Petraglia.) These young ladies from the Donegan School Girl Scout Troop costumed themselves for a play about good nutrition. Little Miss Sunbeam Bread, 10-year-old Clara Nagy, grew up on the South Side and in 1958 married George Petraglia, with whom she raised four children. The troop members from left to right are: (sitting) Patricia Kotlik and Delores Herczeg; (front row) Dorothy Mayer, Helen Mandic, Rosemarie Unger, Beverly Gall, Catherine Ortwein, Gloria Rosati, Maryann Kressler, Patricia Cmorey, and Marion Zelko; (back row) Clary Nagy, Rosemarie Zelko, Anna Marie Mandic, Anna Zaun, and Catherine Berg.

Three

Work

Mr. and Mrs. Charles Schwab, Fiftieth Wedding Anniversary. (Robert Hunsicker.) Charles Schwab married Emma Eurora Dinkey on May 1, 1883, at age 21. Once an engineer's helper earning $1.00 a day, he established Bethlehem Steel Corporation in 1904. He and his wife never had any children, but certainly lived in style, surrounding themselves with lavish homes, fine books, and paintings. On May 1, 1933, Charles and Emma celebrated their fiftieth wedding anniversary at their French chateau on Riverside Drive in Manhattan. It covered an entire city block between 73rd and 74th Streets. Apparently, charitable causes as well as a "policy of welcoming losses as a means of reducing heavy income taxes and lifelong habits of lavish spending reduced and eventually depleted even Schwab's resources." Both Schwab and his wife died, insolvent, in 1939.

Lunchtime, Bessemer Mill Office, Bethlehem Iron Company, 1897. (Tina Juckett.) Harry Stofflett, center, was born in Reading, Pennsylvania, to parents of French and German descent. The family moved to Allentown when he was just ten. Though he attended Lehigh University, the death of his father forced Harry to drop out and go to work at the Bethlehem Iron Company at age 21, after completing a correspondence course in engineering. He remained with the company after it became Bethlehem Steel in 1904 and until his retirement at age 79.

Steelworkers, Bessemer Furnace, Bethlehem Iron Company, 1890. (Lucille and Jack McGinnis.) On a daily basis, these men worked with molten steel at extremely high temperatures in the Bessemer Furnace of the Bethlehem Iron Company. The Bessemer Process was patented by the English inventor Sir Henry Bessemer in 1855. In this process, molten pig iron is poured into a large vessel, called a bessemer converter, and air is blown through the metal, expelling most impurities in the form of gas or as slag. This process was instrumental in pushing the Industrial Revolution forward, as it made steel-making relatively inexpensive and fast, and the process helped make the production of engineering steel and the construction of railroads on a wide scale more feasible.

Volk Boarding House family and steelworker residents, near Hayes Street and Daly Avenue, 1897. (Justina F. Mitala.) Mom and Pop Volk were both from Hungary. They opened their home to boarders, who in this photograph had just come off a shift at the Steel, even though the Volks had eight children of their own to shelter. Pop Volk, standing at the far right, also worked at the Steel. Mom Volk, on the porch, left, is standing next to her daughter Stella, who grew up to marry Patrick A. Ferry, a steel worker who hailed from the coal regions near Eckly. Stella and Patrick lived in Bethlehem and raised seven children.

Visit of Prince Fushimi of Japan to Bethlehem Steel, 1904. (Mrs. Willard Shelly.) His Royal Highness Fushimi, cousin to the Emperor, and his entourage visited Bethlehem Steel on November 30, 1904. Japan's interest in the steel-making process was no doubt piqued by their war with Russia and the Steel's reputation as a maker of artillery and armor plate. The *Globe* reported that the "Prince and suite . . . were shown through the forging, open hearth, steel casting, armor plate, No. 2 machine shop, and other departments of the works. The Prince was much impressed with the magnitude of the works and the ponderous work done."

State constabulary on duty, Bethlehem Steel Company strike, 1910. (Janet Housenick.) At the request of Eugene Grace, Governor Edwin E. Stewart sent twenty-five state constables to Bethlehem to protect the steel plant and scabs from striking workers. Assisted by the International Association of Machinists and the American Federation of Labor, the strikers published a broadside identifying and denouncing those "Notorious Scabs" as "Men who deserted their friends and fellow workers during the great campaign . . . against the Bethlehem Steel Company for living conditions and against Industrial Slavery. What Benedict Arnold was to his country so may these men be known as traitors to the cause of labor the world over."

Iron Foundry Department, Bethlehem Plant, Bethlehem Steel Company, 1921. (Martin Schaffer.) Nearly thirty years after this photo was taken, the Bethlehem Steel Company published a "brief non-technical treatise describing the fundamentals of steelmaking." Of pouring the ingots it said, "After the steel . . . has been tapped from the furnace, the ladle is carried by crane to the pouring platform where a row of ingot molds, usually mounted on cars, is ready to be filled . . . When one mold is filled . . . the ladle is moved over the next mold where the operation is repeated." After the ingots reached the appropriate temperature, they would be removed from the molds and processed by either rolling, hammering, or pressing.

Open House Day, people viewing stockpiled ingots, Saucon Plant, Bethlehem Steel Company, 1917. (Martin Schaffer.) Most likely an exercise in civic virtue and patriotism, Bethlehem Steel staged an open house during the height of World War I. And they had much to be proud of. During the Great War, "Steel mills produced record amounts of shells, armor plate, naval ordnance, ammunition. Orders for steel from Britain, France, and Russia established the American steel industry on the international scene." Bethlehem Steel benefitted greatly from the need for arms; between 1914 and 1918, the Steel's production tripled from 1 million tons to 3 million tons a year.

Chemical laboratory and staff, Bethlehem Steel Corporation, 1925. (Dallam E. Blandy.) The chemical laboratory pictured above was located at the Lehigh Plant, west of the Steel's main plant in Bethlehem. Alloy and tool steel was made there, and the technicians pictured were responsible for analyzing each and every batch of steel produced. This photograph fell into the hands of Dallam Blandy, who arrived in Bethlehem in 1952 and worked at the Steel for thirty-two years. An engineering graduate of Rensselaer Polytechnic Institute, Dallam was the chief chemist at the Bethlehem Plant for the two and a half years prior to his retirement in 1985.

Bethlehem Steel Company Plant patrol force, circa 1941–45. (Marie Schaffer.) Mildred Fritz, left, and Helen Geiger, right, inspect a worker's lunch kit for any "suspicious-looking articles." R.A. Lewis, general manager of the Bethlehem plant, told the *Bethlehem Globe Times*, "We are assigning these women to plant patrol duty to fill vacancies in the force that have been created as some of its members have entered the service or gone into production work. The use of women on the patrol force in assignments that they are qualified to fill makes it possible for just so many more men to continue at other war work in which women might not be as adaptable as men." They were just two of the over 2,000 women who worked at the Bethlehem plant during the Second World War.

Steelworkers on strike, Third Street near main entrance, 1946. (Edward Tumminello.) A no-strike pledge during the war and steady jobs providing plenty of overtime meant relative industrial peace from 1941 to 1945. Yet in 1946 alone, 4.5 million workers participated in nearly five thousand strikes throughout many U.S. industries. Continued government involvement in steel prices and threats by President Truman to take control of several industries led workers to respond with propaganda posters like the one pictured above, reminding the public of Adolph Hitler, who had outlawed unions and regulated wages, production, and working hours in Germany.

Bethlehem Steel Company strike, 1946. (Michael Stofko.) Driving sleet and snow may have slowed down traffic, but not the steelworkers of Bethlehem who took to the picket lines on January 20, 1946, to protest for wage increases as compensation for overtime lost during reconversion. Michael Stofko, left, had been a member of the Steel Workers Organizing Committee during the violent strike of 1941, and he was back on strike five years later with the United Steel Workers of America. The strike of '46 ended on February 15th with workers receiving a raise of 18¢ per hour and the industry securing a $5.00 per ton increase.

Cigar factory workers, 1912. (Mary T. Pongracz.) In the early part of the twentieth century, Bethlehem was the home to about eight different cigar manufacturing concerns. This photograph was taken at Bondy and Lederer's, located at the corner of Buttonwood and Linden Streets. Many young steelworkers' widows, with no other means of support, were compelled to enter the factory. Theresa Zampra Doncsecz Pinter emigrated from Hungary to the United States and settled in South Bethlehem with her steelworker husband. After his death in 1912, Theresa, at age 24, was forced to enter the factory, leaving her youngest child of four with a wet nurse.

Hosiery workers, Philadelphia Hosiery Company, 1915. (Mrs. Robert H. Stewart.) In 1915, there were seven silk and three hosiery manufacturing concerns which served as the female equivalents to Bethlehem Steel, where South Side women and young girls could find production-type jobs. In 1910, the Philadelphia Hosiery Company purchased and expanded a building in Bethlehem which had originally housed a company that produced chenille curtains. The Bethlehem women made hosiery, yet at the Allentown branch, ladies produced woolen dress goods. The Bethlehem mill's yearly production topped $100,000.

Kradjel's Butcher Shop, Anna and Eva Kradjel, Second and Webster Streets, 1915. (Caroline Kinney.) Joseph Kradjel and his wife Anna owned and operated their butcher shop at 102 East Second Street and provided the neighborhood with fresh, choice cuts of meat every day. They resided at the same address with family members Anna, Eva, Joseph, Josephine, and Peter. By 1917, Anna and Joseph had converted their butcher shop to a grocery that, in a time before large supermarkets, was one of nearly 150 groceries in the Bethlehem area.

Bethlehem Fabricators office staff, 1929. (Mildred Leamon Freeman.) Mildred Leamon began working as a receptionist for Bethlehem Fabricators at the age of 16 or 17 and remained there for seven years. Born in White Haven in May 1907, Mildred moved to the South Side with her parents after her father went to work at Bethlehem Steel. Mildred met and fell in love with Fritz Leamon, a draftsman for "the Fabs." She recalls that when they were married, Fritz had only two payments left on his automobile, on which Mildred, far right, and several other office girls are posing for this photograph.

Lunch break, Al Keiserman and Constant E. Young, East Third Street, 1905. (Nancy L. Schmoyer Youst.) Brothers-in-law, Al Keiserman (on the left) and Constant Young, stopped for some lunch at a bakery on East Third Street in South Bethlehem in 1905. Al was married to Constant's sister Savannah, and they boarded with her parents, Clinton and Mattie, at 423 Pawnee Street. At the time, Al was a laborer with the Philadelphia and Reading Railroad and Constant was a student. Constant, who married his wife May in 1913, later worked as a clerk for the Bethlehem Steel Company.

Becker's Saloon, Jacob Becker, Main Street, 1910. (Louise Becker Rittoper.) Jacob Becker, born in the province of Hesse, Germany, arrived in America with his parents, Jacob Sr. and Gertrude, when he was two years old. Mr. Becker was the treasurer of the Beethoven Maennerchor for fifteen years. Though he never held any public office, he served as a member of the Northampton County Law and Order League and "took great interest in public affairs." Mr. Becker worked in the retail liquor business for thirty-eight years in Bethlehem, retiring at age 60, only a few weeks before his death in 1913.

44

Wallace Bloom, justice of the peace, Third Street, South Bethlehem, 1912. (Marion Schnalzer.) Wallace Bloom was a justice of the peace for South Bethlehem around 1910 and saw much action during the steel strike of that year. Wallace had married Ellen Miller Bloom, and they had three children, Maude, Frank, and George. Ellen, sadly, died in 1904. Wallace then married Elvina Haney. After serving as the justice of the peace, Wallace held several different positions, finally settling in as a clerk for the Bethlehem Steel Company in 1917.

Seltzer and Sons delivery truck driven by George Ritter, 1917. (Gertrude Ritter Laubach.) George Ritter worked for George E. Seltzer, owner of Seltzer and Sons Furniture, from after 1912 into the early 1920s, when the business closed. George, who resided at 153 Cunow Street with his wife Lizzie, had delivered goods for a number of Bethlehem businesses over the years. Early in the century, he worked as a driver for Aaron B. Levers, a brick manufacturer, and then as a teamster for the Artificial Ice Company. Following his time with Seltzer and Sons, George, like so many Bethlehemites, took a position with the Bethlehem Steel Corporation.

Lowering the casket, Kinney Funeral Home (1910–1920), South Bethlehem, 1915. (Charles and Jean Downing.) Memorial services completed, the casket of a young woman is lowered from the window of the room in which she expired. The body of the deceased was prepared for burial in the home; the casket was brought up the stairs and afterward brought down by a system of pulleys. Waiting below is the white coach and the white horses that drew the casket to the cemetery. The Kinney Funeral Home owned two sets of coaches, a white one for young women and children, and a black one, drawn by black horses, for others.

Funeral, Kinney Funeral Home staff and mourners, South Bethlehem. (Charles and Jean Downing) Joseph Kinney, far right, arrived in Bethlehem in May of 1889 and established his business in South Bethlehem when he was twenty years old. Hailing from the coal regions to the north, Joseph operated Kinney Funeral Home until the early 1920s, when his son-in-law Herbert M. Downing joined him. Joseph passed away in 1931, after forty-two years in Bethlehem. Herbert M. Downing changed the name of the funeral home to Downing Funeral Home, and his son, Charles, who joined the business in 1969, became the proprietor in May 1990.

East End Marble and Granite Works, Webster Street, 1910. (Lucille and Jack McGinnis.) Frank P. McGinnis, proprietor of East End Marble and Granite, and his son John were skilled stonecutters who provided a valuable service to the citizens of Bethlehem. While funeral director Joseph Kinney helped the families and friends say good-bye to their loved ones, the McGinnis men created beautiful stone monuments as enduring legacies to the deceased for decades to come.

Globe carriers, Curt (on left) and Harry Ihle, 1054 Jeter Avenue, 1922. (Deborah L. Sobrinski.) No matter the weather or the temperature, Curt and Harry Ihle arose before sunrise every morning to deliver the 2¢ an issue *Bethlehem Globe*. Their mother Clara always had a warm breakfast and dry clothes waiting for them at home before they had to head for school. Curt, born in 1910, graduated from Liberty High School and held a position in the offices of Bethlehem Steel. He also played Santa Claus for thirty years for the CYO. Harry was born in 1908; a graduate of the Fountain Hill School, he worked as a pattern maker at Tredwell in Easton and loved to attend Jolly Joe Timmer polkas.

Grosh's Confectionery, Herman S. Grosh Sr. and relations, Broad Street, 1882. (Elizabeth Weller Wall.) Elizabeth Myers, in her newspaper column "Nature, History and Other Lore," took *Daily Times* readers on a walk down memory lane to Bethlehem's "Ice Cream Parlors of Long Ago." She wrote fondly of Grosh's Confectionery and its proprietor, Herman S. Grosh. "Grosh made his own ice cream and candies and his shop was a favorite place for the school children and Seminary girls. His ice cream was the pure stuff, no modern powders or gelatins to thicken it in a hurry, and his candies were of the same quality. Those large trays of sugary coconut candy still linger in the memory and almost in the taste!"

Tow truck, Garvin I. Moyer, Allen Motor Company, Fifth Avenue at Broad Street, 1930. (Garvin E. Kram.) Garvin Kram recalls helping his uncle Garvin Moyer as a little kid, cleaning up the place and driving this 1926 Essex tow truck around the yard of the Allen Motor Company. Garvin Moyer began working for the repair shop at a young age as a washboy greasing cars. Around 1940, he became the owner of the business, which specialized in repairs and the selling of Essex and Hudson autos. As a matter of fact, the car pictured above belonged to a Dr. Biddleman, who attended the birth of Garvin Kram.

Meilinger's Store, Irene and Paul E. Meilinger Sr., 610 East Third Street, 1935. (Mary M. Meilinger.) Irene Takacs, born in Winnipeg, Manitoba, Canada, started working as a clerk at Meilinger's Cigar Store on East Third Street when she was just fourteen. After her marriage to Paul Meilinger, she continued to work and operate the store, selling cigars, tobacco, popular magazines, and cameras, until her retirement in 1945.

Mowrer's Ice Cream, Frank Mohap, Broadway in Fountain Hill, 1938. (John L. Mohap.) Frank Mohap was born on September 1, 1919, to Frank and Anna Czor Mohap. In 1938, at age 19, Frank worked for Mowrer's Ice Cream store while he attended school. Frank lived at home on North Hoffert Street in Fountain Hill with his widowed mother, who ran a grocery from the same address. Frank, who served in the military during both World War II and the Korean War, married Margaret Svanda on June 22, 1942, and together they raised three sons. A data processor for Bethlehem Steel, he retired in 1981.

Mowrer's milkman, Anthony J. Hutnick, 1953. (Kathleen Hutnick.) Anthony Hutnick was born and raised in Nazareth, Pennsylvania. His first job was as a projectionist at a movie house in Nazareth. In 1947, he married Mary Yost, and they moved to Bethlehem when Anthony got a new job at the Palace Theatre. In the early 1950s, Anthony started working for Mowrer's delivering Golden Guernsey milk. He stayed with the company for sixteen years. He and Mary raised two daughters, Kathleen Hutnick and Anne Hutnick Sisle.

Horninger's Gas Station, Stephen M. Horninger, Third and Evans Streets, 1940. (Rosanne Bridges.) In 1939, Stephen Horninger married his wife Amelia, who he met while delivering milk to her parents' grocery. A man who loved everything he ever did, Stephen was a hard worker. Stephen, born in 1919, not only worked for thirty years as a laborer at the Steel, but also at the gas station. He owned Horninger's Restaurant on Union Boulevard and Maple Vending Company, a bubble gum machine outfit, and even ran concessions at Willow Park during the summer.

Pappas Bros. Store, George Pappas, 1951. (George and Anne Pappas.) The Pappas Brothers Store was founded by George Pappas' father Hercules and his uncle James. George eventually took over the store and kept the original name. Pappas Brothers was located at the corner of Columbia and New Streets and was not only a successful grocery, but also a popular deli. Local steelworkers would drop in on a daily basis for a bag lunch. This photograph was taken four years prior to Hurricane Diane. After that storm, George found himself with 17 inches of water in the store and a completely flooded cellar. The store was sold to make way for the Fahy Bridge.

Klausen's Shoe Repair, Niels Klausen, 1935 W. Broad Street, 1981. (Norma A. Beck.) Niels Klausen arrived in the United States from Denmark in 1921, at age 16. Quickly relieved by a pickpocket of the "three or four bucks" he had borrowed for his trip, Niels joined his brother Bertel in the shoe repair trade. In 1928, Niels married Mildred Bright, who worked in the silk mills until the first of their seven children arrived. He retired in 1983, after sixty-two years of repairing shoes for the people of Bethlehem.

Four

Recreation

Bach Choir of Bethlehem on steps of Central Moravian Church, 1903. (Bach Choir of Bethlehem.) The Bach Festival of 1903 opened on May 11th at the Central Moravian Church, and the *Globe* appears to have approved of the first performance. "Just as the king of day in all his matchless glory down-sloped in the west, the mellow tones of the trombone choir floated out from the belfry of the old church, flooding the . . . avenues and reminding one strangely of the Bayreuth of old. Bethlehem became as a Leaf from the Past, a faded page of two centuries ago, but written over musically with firmer hand and surer manner in the matter of interpretation than was even possible in Bach's time."

Pioneer Drum Corps, South Bethlehem, 1909. (Esther M. Frisoli.) The Pioneer Drum Corps lent its services to many a celebration and parade through the streets of Bethlehem. George Overdorf (first row, third from the left) was a member of the drum corps as a young man. Born in 1896 in Wilkes Barre, he was only thirteen when this photograph was taken. He moved to Bethlehem with his mother and remained in the city his entire life, except when he went west to Kansas to find his fortune. Quickly discovering he was not cut out for the climate or the cornfields, he returned to Bethlehem via the undercarriages of trains heading east. Broke financially, but not spiritually, he vowed never to be poor again. He married Bella Roberts in 1917, raised eleven children, and made a career at Lehigh Valley Railroad.

Musicians for season with Morton Opera Company, Central Park, 1912. (William Poczak.) On May 25, 1912, the *Globe* reported that "Central Park Theater had an auspicious opening for the current season . . . and the initial bill by the Morton Opera Company was presented in a style that was altogether pleasing and that proved to the satisfaction of the large audience." For 10¢, 20¢, and 30¢, park-goers could enjoy matinees or evening performances, all accompanied by the musicians pictured above.

Moravian Trombone Choir, Bach Festival, outside Packer Chapel, Lehigh University, 1923.
(Robert T. Brown.) The Moravian Trombone Choir accompanied the Bach Choir to Hershey,
Pennsylvania, in June of 1923, in celebration of that town's twentieth anniversary. Before each
concert by the Bach Choir, attended by record-breaking crowds, the trombonists, "directed by
George Sigley, played chorale tunes on the outside of the auditorium for nearly a half hour,
thousands gathering nearby to hear this traditional music."

**Bethlehem Steel Company Band at Lehigh University, entrance to Linderman Library,
1927.** (Robert H. Daugherty.) On December 23, 1910, the citizens of the city lined the streets
and the shopkeepers bedecked their establishments with bunting and banners in anticipation
of Charles M. Schwab's band's premier public appearance. Employees of the Steel, the band "in
uniform was attractive, the musicians being to an individual typical specimens of the brawn and
alertness of the several iron and steel working trades and professions." Jim the pony, who carted
the bass drum, belonged to Director Weingartner and had been "secured . . . to lessen the labor
of the artist who extracts the music from that cumbersome instrument."

Bethlehem Symphony Orchestra, Leonard J. Luckenbach, director, first concert, Liberty High School, 1924. (Mrs. Leonard J. Luckenbach.) Leonard J. Luckenbach was born in Bethlehem to Jacob and Ida Stubblebine Luckenbach and was a founding member and director of the Bethlehem Symphony Orchestra. Leonard was an avid violinist and a member of the Bach Choir. Besides his reputation as a musician, Leonard had the honor of being known as quite a craftsman. In 1937, he designed the city's first official Christmas putz depicting the birth of Jesus Christ. Mr. Luckenbach was a sales engineer for the Fuller Company in Catasauqua until his retirement in 1966.

Bethlehem Steel Company Band rehearsal, second floor, Band Building (old library), Market Street, 1920. (Fern Koplin.) When Charles M. Schwab came up with the idea of a company band, he was adamant in his requirements. As supplier of the instruments and uniforms for the band, Schwab demanded the highest quality from those who would be the musicians. He is reported to have said in 1910, "I want the band to be the best in the Lehigh Valley, and it's going to be that or I'll have none of it." Ten years later, the band was still going strong.

Union Bricklayers Band of Bethlehem, Local #8, 1920. (Carl W. Cool.) The Bricklayers Union Local #8 was started in Bethlehem in 1896, and it supported the labor interests of local contractors and journeymen. It also served as an almost fraternal organization for its members, bringing men of common interest together not only for work concerns, but also for recreation. George Cool, born in 1863, came to Bethlehem from the coal regions and went to work as a bricklayer and became a member and musician for Local #8. George's six sons also entered the trade, as did his grandson, Carl. The last Cool to take up the profession is Carl's nephew, Jimmy Stametz.

Beethoven Maennerchor, Union Station, 1914. (Betty Gross Riter.) On October 23, 1874, soon after the organization of the Beethoven Maennerchor, the *Daily Times* wished the "newly organized band of vocalists every possible success and encouragement." By 1914, trips out of town for conventions and vocal competitions were not rare. Even today, nearly 125 years later, the Maennerchor is still going strong. Now known as the Beethoven Choruses, the group meets regularly on Wednesday evenings for practice and continues to perform and compete. The trophies that line the walls of their clubhouse in Hellertown attest to the group's success.

The Pastime Social Club, Jersey Central Station, 1885. (Sandra P. McKinney.) The Pastime Social Club gathered together for a group photograph on the platform of the Central Rail Road of New Jersey. In 1895, it appears that the club ran into a little bit of trouble. Only six months after moving its headquarters to South Bethlehem, it was "rumored that the Pastime Social Club, that had quartered in the Peysert Building at the Five Points, moved their household and bric-a-brac to parts unknown . . . Rumors of arrest for the recovery of sums due are prevalent."

Race track, Bethlehem Fairgrounds, Linden Street area, 1899. (George Vasko.) On the second day of the 1899 fall race season of the Pennsylvania State Fair Association at Bethlehem, Prince Alert won a $1,000 purse and smashed the world record with a half-mile race of 2.06 minutes flat. The *Globe* took the opportunity to profess Bethlehem's track the "finest half-mile track ever built in the confines of this grand old Commonwealth of ours." And of course the paper took the opportunity to rub it in that Prince Alert smashed the record previously set on Allentown's home track. "How silently the half hundred Allentown fellows marched from the fairgrounds . . . Upon their countenances was depicted the deepest disgust. . . . [The] shock to those sports was really pathetic to the extreme."

58

Cycling Club, 1890. (Barbara Fowler.) Many cycling clubs established in the United States in the late nineteenth century were formal affairs modeled on the U.S. Cavalry. Incorporated as virtuous organizations, cycling clubs were considered "centers for the active, healthy growth of a more vigorous form of democracy." As witnessed by their military-style dress, the Alpha Wheel men were dedicated to this expansion of American ideals. The buglers would call assembly at dawn, and the riders would gather in front of the club's headquarters at 33 S. New Street. Pulling out in formation, they would be off for a ride through the streets of the city and on into the countryside.

Original members of Slovak Gymnastic Union, Sokol Lodge #93, 1915. (Joseph B. Raykos.) A Notice of Incorporation for the Slovak Gymnastic Union appeared in the *Globe* in February of 1910. It announced that members of the Slovak community desired to establish a union modeled after those from the old country for "the practice of all kinds of gymnastic exercises and the promotion of all kinds of athletic sports." The original members of Sokol Lodge #93 are from left to right: (first row) John Stofko, Steve Novotny, John Baran, Joe Barron, and Adam Kuruc; (back row) Emil Davco, Steve Cuchran, Joe Sopko, and Mike Glagola.

Packer Athletic Club football team, 1904. (Merritt F. Weaver.) Formed for recreation and physical fitness, sports organizations also felt the occasional sting of tragedy. On November 19, 1904, a player in a match between Hellertown and the Packer A.C. received a "concussion of the brain and sustained injuries to the peritoneum, which caused his death." The *Globe*, usually supportive in its reporting of local teams, lashed out at the sport. "The player . . . is dead as the result of the inherent brutality and dangerousness of the game of football . . . There was the usual ensemble of players, the secret code of signals for combinations, the usual cheers and applause and—the tragic end."

East End baseball team, East End Field, 1906. (Mr. and Mrs. Paul Clay.) On Saturday, September 15, over 1,800 spectators witnessed East End's nine players deliver a rousing defeat of 5-1 to the West Siders in the final game of the Bethlehem City League's 1906 season. With victory, the East Ends brought home the City League pennant and a prize of $100. Assembling at the Brighton Hotel on New Street at 8 pm, the Bethlehem Band, the Pioneer Drum Corps, the players, and hundreds of fans danced through the city streets in an impromptu parade, as spectators cheered and fireworks lit the sky.

Bethlehem Steel Company baseball team, Steel Field, 1915. (Ray D. Gold.) The *Globe* reported, on June 10, 1910, that a "team which is at once expected to show good form and capture the local pennant has been organized from the employees of the Bethlehem Steel Works . . . Rumor already has it that after this bunch of 'stars' gets playing together they will be as fast as 'Halley's Comet.'" In their first home game, "an exceptionally interesting game," they defeated the boys from Catasauqua, 1-0.

Hungarian soccer players, South Bethlehem, 1917. (Elsie Yelenics Schupp.) Ethnic groups in Bethlehem formed their own soccer teams and usually played against other ethnic teams from the South Side. According to Armindo Sousa, whose Portuguese-American Club still has a soccer team, early in the century it was the Hungarian, Irish, Portuguese, and Germans who ranked as the best of the ethnic leagues.

61

Bethlehem Steel Company soccer team, National Champions, 1918. (L.D. Sheridan.) On May 19, 1918, the Bethlehem Steel Company soccer team clinched the National Cup Championship at Federal League Ball Park in Newark, New Jersey, by a score of 3-0. The June 3rd issue of the *Bethlehem Steel* reported that "the game, from the start, was fast and scientific, and it did not take long for the large crowd to appreciate that the Bethlehem boys outclassed the Fall River Rovers in every stage of the game." Coach Harry W. Trend's team established an impressive record of 162 wins, 6 losses, and 16 ties between the 1913 and 1919 seasons.

North End Football Club, 1919. (Pat Zulli Jr.) The Blue Mountain Soccer League began its 1918–1919 season on December 23rd. The *Globe* announced just one week later that "the teams are rapidly rounding into form and that the competition for supremacy is gradually tightening." The North Ends prevailed. On March 15, 1919, they secured the H.E. Lewis Cup in a victory over the Saucon Cross Roads by a score of 2-1. Nearly a month later, another match between the same teams, this time for the Warren A. Wilbur cup, resulted in a 1-0 victory by the North Ends, but only after two extra 15-minute periods. "The playing of the two teams was probably the best witnessed in that circuit this season and kept the fans on the edge from the very start to the finish."

National Theatre, 1910. (Lucy Tomanio.) A nickel gained entrance to Angelo Tocce's National Moving Picture Theater, 72 Broad Street, in 1909. An advertisement in the *Globe* boasted the supremacy of the National Theater. "Every picture produced here is a feature picture, for the simple reason that you can look at these pictures without experiencing that intoxicating sensation, because there is no 'flickering' or 'flashing' while the picture is in motion. Come and be convinced." In addition to motion pictures, illustrated songs were performed daily by the "popular baritone, John L. Beckler."

Offices of the Broad Theatre, Thomas W. Heiberger, manager, Broad Street, 1917. (Marjorie L. Heiberger.) Thomas Heiberger managed the family-owned Broad Theatre, while his father Lorenzo took care of business down the road at the Lorenz, 37 Broad Street. In 1917, Bethlehemites had a wide variety of theatrical entertainment from which to choose, such as *The Golden Idiot*, the story of "how a beloved vagabond takes a 1000-to-1 chance for a fortune and wins it, as well as the love of a pretty heiress," playing at the Lehigh Orpheum. Or perhaps *The Bar Sinister*, "a red-blooded drama with tremendous climaxes," playing down at the Palace.

Canoeing on the Lehigh Canal, 1920. (Thomas J. Cunningham.) The Lehigh Canal originally ran for 46.2 miles from Mauch Chunk to Easton and later expanded as far north as White Haven. The primary traffic were coal-laded barges, although other freight was also hauled. By the 1920s, when this photograph was taken, Lehigh Coal and Navigation had lost much of its freight traffic to the railroads, but the canal began to attract outdoor enthusiasts who either cruised its waters or biked along its edge. The Depression dealt the final blow, although Lehigh Coal and Navigation continued to own the canal into the 1960s. Today it is part of the Delaware and Lehigh Navigation Canal National Corridor.

Bowling team, YWCA, 1929. (Kathleen A. Widner/Carolyn S. Emrich.) During the 1928–29 bowling season, the competition between the twelve YWCA Pin League teams was "keen in lieu of the honors that [would] be given and prizes awarded the teams and individuals who [attained] the highest scores throughout the winter and spring." On February 25, 1929, the "Lassies" of Team Four were giving the other eleven teams a run for the money, as they "captured the high score of the evening and marked one more successful stride toward winning the high team honors." Their score of 1,037 was nearly 150 points higher than their closest rival's score.

Summer street entertainer with live bear, East Fourth Street, South Bethlehem, 1900. (Mr. and Mrs. Dale R. Lee.) Even though life in the mills and factories of the South Side was hard, there were often bright spots and moments of merriment when entertainers, such as this man and his bear, came to town. In the early part of the century, residents were enthralled by acts from Pawnee Bill's Wild West Show, J.H. La Pearl's Colossal Circus and Hippodrome, and even the famous Ringling Brothers' World's Greatest Show with "1,000 people, 40 Famous Funny Clowns, 50 Musicians in Grand Popular Preliminary Concerts, 5 Big Arenas, . . . 65 Railroad Cars, [and] 100 Dens, Lairs and Cages of Rare Wild Beasts."

Playing shuffle board, YWCA, 1946. (Mildred E. Aungst.) The YWCA of Bethlehem drew many teenagers to its building at New and Market Streets. An organization dedicated to building strong character in young ladies, the "Y" also provided them with recreational activities. It was a place where young Joan Beehler and Mildred Mac Murtrie learned how to play a mean game of shuffle board. Still close friends, Millie and Joan graduated from Liberty High School in 1950. Joan now lives in Arkansas. Millie and her husband Clinton Aungst raised two daughters in Bethlehem, and Millie retired from the Bethlehem Area Public Library in April 1997, after twenty-eight years of service.

Chapter members, Bethal Lodge #1284, Elks Home, 1960. (Mrs. Dorothy S. Johnson.) The Improved Benevolent and Protective Order of Elks of the World (IBPOEW) came into existence in 1897. The black counterpart to the once all-white Benevolent and Protective Order of Elks, the IBPOEW was created to promote "the expression of ideals, services, and leadership in the black struggle for freedom and opportunity." Established in Bethlehem in the 1940s, the Bethal Lodge #1284 is located at 316 Brodhead and still meets twice a month.

Wyoming Lodge #135, Masonic Lodge, 1965. (Mrs. Lillian C. Taylor.) Wyoming Lodge #135 was established in Bethlehem in 1927 by Ross Washington, a laborer for the Bethlehem Steel Corporation. Major Williams, who was kind of enough to provide this information, has been a member of both the Wyoming Lodge and the Bethal Lodge for over fifty years. Major arrived in Bethlehem with his wife Mary in 1943. Hailing from Albany, Georgia, Major came to the city during World War II knowing he would find work at the Steel. He remained with the company for almost thirty-six years, retiring from the Saucon Rolling Shop in 1978.

Edgeboro Women's Democratic Club, Fourth Club Anniversary, 1965. (Anna A. Stofko.) Interested women got together in the early 1960s and established the Edgeboro Women's Democratic Club. Not feminists in the traditional sense, these were politically-minded, politically-aware women who worked hard to get their candidates known and elected to office. They are, from left to right: (sitting) Hilda McFall, Jeannete Riebman (who went on to become a state senator), Agnes Smerko, Christine Spevak, Wilma Matus, Anna Ruyak (president), Anna Stofko, and Helen Kmita; (standing) Mary Zabrecky, unidentified, Mary Hays, Jennie Holletz, Agnes Corcione, Ann Danner, and Helen Sutton.

Maclaren Pipe and Drum Band, 1970. (Fred Gilmartin.) Descendants of the Scotch-Irish settlers to the Lehigh Valley continue to celebrate and preserve their heritage as much as those families who arrived in the late nineteenth and early twentieth centuries. The first Celts in the Lehigh Valley arrived in the eighteenth century after escaping famines and the economic collapse of Ulster. Local groups, such as the Maclaren Pipe and Drum Band, celebrate their ancestry year-round. The MacLaren Pipe and Drum Band share a culture rich in song and dance and also feast with the other groups of the Valley at the Celtic Classic, which is entering its tenth year in Bethlehem in 1997.

Portuguese-American Club, Folklore Group, Brodhead Avenue, 1975. (Armindo P. Sousa.) Originally finding work in the zinc and coal mines to the north, many Portuguese moved to South Bethlehem to find work at the Steel. Armindo Sousa's father arrived from Portugal in 1914. He left a good job in a bakery when he heard of the jobs and money to be made in the states. He went back to Portugal for a time but returned to Bethlehem following his marriage. The Portuguese community is still active and boasts about 5,000 members.

Tatra Slovak Folk Group, Ss. Cyril and Methodius Hall, 1977. (Mary Stofanak.) In 1977, a group of Bethlehemites formed the Tatra Slovak Folk Group, whose primary aim is the preservation of the Slovak heritage through traditional dance, song, and clothing. The original members are pictured above. From left to right are: (front row) Irene Horvath, Mary Stofanak, William Macek Jr., Patricia Timko, and Mary Pavlinsky; (second row) William Macek Sr., Marge Posivak, Lillian Vasko, Tom Klopack, Lucille Majewski, Marge Fidmik, and Betty Nemchik; (third row) Anna Mae Klopack, Elizabeth Jasso, Stan Majewski, Mary Shannon, Steve Farris, Anna Adamcik, and Anna Macek; (back row) Marie Cavote, Joe Nemchik, Mike Krajci, Marge Brozman, Ed Shannon, and Tom Stofko.

Five

Faith

Harvest Service, St. Thomas Lutheran and Reformed Church, Macada Road, 1898.
(William B. Stecker.) Originally called St. Thomas Monaquacy Church, the St. Thomas
Lutheran and Reformed Church was organized in 1848. On the cornerstone, laid on May 30,
1846, it reads, "RESOLVED, That each of the two congregations shall have every alternate
Sunday to its free and undisturbed use. RESOLVED, That neither of the congregations shall
have an advantage over the other in title or right . . . nor be allowed to disturb the other in its
religious worship." In 1971, the Lutheran congregation chose to consolidate with St. Thomas
United Church of Christ.

Easter Morning Service, God's Acre, Moravian Cemetery, 1890. (Margaret Sattler.) "Out upon the night air, while the stars shone bright and the full-orbed moon stood still to listen, sounded the solemn music of the Moravian trombones proclaiming the risen Lord . . . Hundreds of worshippers arose at the sound of the grave, sweet psalmody. The pavements re-echoed with many a footfall . . . Out into the graveyard as the sun was beginning to shoot its shafts far across the sky the procession of more than 2,000 worshippers wended its way. The deep-voiced trombones were pouring forth a sweet old German choral."

Celebration, St. John's Windish Lutheran Church, East Fourth Street, 1914. (St. John's Windish Lutheran Church.) The Windish came to Bethlehem from Slovenia in the first decade of this century. Though most were Catholic, the Protestant Windish founded St. John's Windish Lutheran Church in 1910. Originally, the church was called St. John's Evangelical Lutheran Slovenian Church, and its members worshiped in St. Peter's Lutheran Church until 1911 while they readied their own House of God. The photograph above was taken when Ernest A. Steigler, whose tenure began July 4, 1914, was pastor of the church.

Laying the cornerstone, St. Joseph's Windish Roman Catholic Church, South Bethlehem, 1914. (Rev. Lawrence Frankovich.) A cause for great celebration, the cornerstone laying of St. Joseph's Windish Roman Catholic Church drew many congregants and a great variety of church officials from as far away as New York City. According to the *Globe*, on the morning of November 8, 1914, the exercises began "in the basement of the Church of the Holy Infancy with a solemn High Mass at which Mgr. Masson [of Allentown] was the celebrant. . . . Mgr. Masson and the visiting priests followed by the various societies of the parish proceeded to the church on Fifth Street, where the cornerstone was laid."

Laying the cornerstone, Brith Sholom Community Center, Packer Avenue and Brodhead, 1924. (Congregation Brith Sholom.) An "epoch-making event," the laying of the Brith Sholom Community Center's cornerstone took place on Sunday, June 15, 1924. The ceremony was attended not only by "men prominent in the Jewish faith but also [by] gentiles of prominence in the religious, business, and civic affairs of the community." A metal box containing the names of the center's board of directors, a copy of the plans, copies of the *Globe* and the *Daily Times*, and brief histories of Brith Sholom Community Center, the YMHA, the Ladies' Aid, the Unity League, and other groups was sealed and the cornerstone cemented into place.

Young men of West Bethlehem Moravian Church, Prospect Street, 1910. (Elsie Yelenics Schupp.) The West Side Moravian Church grew out of the religious good deeds of Moravian Seminary student Joseph Romig, who opened a Sunday school on the west side of the Monocacy in May 1860. Meeting at the Vineyard Street schoolhouse, young seminary students provided religious instruction and guidance to canal boatmen and their children. Beginning service on September 29, 1901, the Reverend F.W. Stengel, who presided at the church when this photograph was taken, was the first pastor of the West Side Moravian Chapel.

Edgeboro Moravian Church, 1930. (Ellen Julian.) Similar to the West Side Moravian Church, the Edgeboro Moravian Church grew out of a Sunday school begun by four Moravian Theological Seminary students. On October 25, 1914, twenty-eight persons assembled for the first Sunday school class; the four seminary students, J. George Bruner, Caclav Vancura, Herbert Kant, and Douglas Rights, held the first worship service in December of that same year. During the 1930s, the Reverend Earl W. Christianson was pastor of the church.

72

Confirmation of Szabo girls, Helen, Magdalena, Betty, and Julia, 1926. (Mary Lou Crocus.)
Helen (on left) and Betty Szabo (second to right) were confirmed at St. John Capistrano
on Fourth Street in 1926. Attending them were godmothers Magdalena (second on the left),
who had eloped to Maryland with their brother John, and Julia (far right), their sister. Sadly,
Betty passed away at an early age. Helen, who was quite involved in Democratic politics later
in life, married steelworker Joseph Burkhardt and had three children: Kathleen, Thomas,
and Mary Louise. Julia married as well and had a large family. Perhaps the most famous member
of the family, who is not pictured, is the Szabo girls' niece, Pat Holetz, Bethlehem's very
own Chicken Lady.

Bishop's visit to St. Nicholas Greek Orthodox Church, East Fourth Street, circa 1922–24. (Emanuel C. Bakis.) Around 1912, Greek immigrants held their first religious services in Bethlehem. They gathered at St. Joseph's Chapel on Fourth Street, which they rented for $35.00 per month from the Episcopal Church of the Nativity. The Greek Orthodox congregation purchased the church in 1917. Sometime between 1922 and 1924, Alexander, the first Archbishop of North and South America, paid a visit to the Bethlehem congregation of St. Nicholas Greek Orthodox Church. Standing to the left of the archbishop is the Reverend John Abraham, who served the parish from 1922 through June 1924. St. Nicholas is now located at 1607 West Union Boulevard.

Confirmation Class, St. Peter's Lutheran Church, Packer Avenue and Vine Street, 1925. (Marlene L. Simons.) A meeting called by the Reverend Augustus Theodosius Geissenhainer in August of 1863 resulted in the first organized Christian congregation on the southern side of the Lehigh River at St. Peter's Lutheran Church. Services were conducted in German well into the twentieth century, though as early as 1873, English is known to have been used. Seated with these young church members is the Reverend James O. Leibensperger. The reverend, who received his Doctor of Divinity from Muhlenberg College in 1925, served the parish from 1901 to 1937.

74

First Communion Class, St. Joseph's Church, East Fifth Street, 1926. (Sheila and Tony Kozo.) Father Clement Veren, O.F.M. and a Windish-Slovenian pastor from Europe, arrived at St. Joseph's in 1923. Father Veren was instrumental in establishing St. Joseph's Parochial School, which opened in 1926. Chances are that most of the children in this photograph attended the parochial school, as their parents would have preferred a school in which their native language was spoken and their heritage preserved. As the decades passed and as youngsters became more "Americanized," enrollment at the school dropped. The school, having only sixty-nine registered students, closed in 1977.

St. Mark Evangelical Church Choir, studio shot, circa 1930. (Donna K. Berge.) In 1888, a meeting called by A.L. Cope and attended by eight others was convened to discuss the establishment of an English-language Lutheran church in South Bethlehem. On December 8, 1895, the church, "one of the most beautiful edifices in the borough," was dedicated. The *Globe* remarked that despite the small size and relative youth of the church, the congregation of St. Mark's had "accomplished great things" and their pride in their edifice was justifiable. By 1937, near the time of this photograph, more than 400 people were baptized members of the church, now located on Easton Avenue.

St. Nicholas Russian Orthodox Church, original members of the Choir Club, East Sixth Street, 1937. (John Frimenko Jr.) Russian Orthodox immigrants from the areas surrounding Minsk, Grodno, and Volhynia founded St. Nicholas Russian Orthodox Church in 1916. During the years of the Great Depression, economic hardships did not dampen the spirit of the congregation. In the church's 75th anniversary publication, it noted that the "steadfast faith and dignified persistence of our priests and our people kept the spirit of the church alive, overcoming obstacles that seemed insurmountable."

St. Nicholas Russian Orthodox Church Dance Troupe, studio shot, 1939. (Kathryn Bilsak.) One of the benefits of living in the United States is the opportunity to learn a great deal about the religions and folk customs belonging to citizens with varying ethnic backgrounds. Churches have always been focal points for many ethnic communities; they provide venues in which traditions are kept alive. This dance troupe attests to the fact that youngsters growing up in the United States could become "American" without losing touch with their ethnic heritages.

St. Mark's Sunday School, Northampton Heights, South Bethlehem, 1929. (Ella M. Siegfried.) According to the cornerstone, St. Mark's Evangelical United Brethren was built in 1905. It was located on what was then Hellertown Road, which later became East Fourth Street, between Anthracite and Bessemer Streets. The pastor in 1929 was the Reverend Quintan Roth. When the Northampton Heights area was redeveloped in preparation for the construction of Bethlehem Steel's basic oxygen furnace, neither the building nor the church organization survived.

Confirmation Class, Grace Lutheran Church, Broad Street, 1930. (Claire E. Hochella.) Though people with strong ties to their homeland did much to hold on to their heritage, often after years in America, out of necessity and desire, they began to speak English both in and out of church. Members of the Salem Lutheran Church, who wanted to hear services conducted in English, formed Grace Lutheran Church in January 1872. Located at 72–73 East Broad Street, the parish house was the birthplace of the Reverend Dr. Franklin Clark Fry, who was president of the Lutheran Church of America. Seated in the photograph with this confirmation class is J. Howard Worth, D.D., who served the church from 1926 to 1946.

First Communion Day — Mildred Lauer, Mary Jane Bringenberg, and Catherine Lauer, Fountain Hill, 1937. (Mrs. Eleanor Bringenberg.) Neighborhood friends, Mildred (on left) and Catherine Lauer (on right) and Mary Jane Bringenberg (center), pose in one of their backyards before heading to St. Ursula's Catholic Church in Fountain Hill for their first communion. Mildred and Catherine were the daughters of Michael, a machinist, and Helen Lauer and lived at 1122 Russell Avenue. Next door was the Bringenberg residence where Mary Jane lived with her parents, Eleanor and Lawrence, and her many brothers and sisters.

Catechetical Class, Emmanuel Evangelical Congregational Church, Center Street and Union Boulevard, 1938. (William H. Reese Jr.) The Emmanuel Evangelical Congregation was often on the move. Originally named St. John's upon its founding in 1853, it met at the Odd Fellows Hall on New Street. A new church was built at New and North Streets in 1854; a second was built at 17 East North Street in 1880; and their third church at 75 East Union Boulevard was dedicated in 1895. The present church was built on the same site in 1912. The Reverend F.G. Yost served as pastor when this photograph was taken in 1938.

St. Peter's Society, East Fourth Street, 1941. (Palma R. Lucia.) Sunday, June 29, 1941, marked the dedicatory ceremony of St. Peter Society's new home at 817–819 East Fourth Street. The Italian-American organization was established in Bethlehem in 1919 by thirty-nine members. Having met for twenty years in the Holy Rosary Church hall, the group, which had grown to over 400 members, needed more room. Their new building contained a banquet and assembly room, a social room with an adjoining kitchen, officers quarters, and cocktail and card rooms. Perhaps best of all were the "bocce alleys of sufficient size to accommodate an indefinite number of people."

Grace Lutheran Church Sunday school, Broad and Center Streets, 1945. (Mrs. Ruth Koehler Boyer Hinkle.) The Sunday school at Grace Lutheran Church was organized on January 5, 1873, the same day of the consecration of the church basement. The initial "enrollment of sixty scholars and teachers" continued to grow and thrive over the years, surviving depressions and wars, and it is still going strong to this day.

Women's Chorus, 1945. (Mrs. Lillian C. Taylor.) Local musician William Rohs provided his musical talents to a group of women from the South Side who loved to sing. Once or twice a week the women would gather at Mr. Rohs' home at 462 Montclair Avenue and practice their songs. Of all different faiths, these ladies joined together for the pure joy of singing. They often showed off their talents at area churches during the holidays, as well as at the local YWCA.

Confirmation Class, Calvary Church, Wood Street, 1952. (Christine H. Simon.) Calvary Church was located on Wood Street in 1952, the year these youngsters were confirmed by the church. From left to right are: (front row) Charlotte Bradford, Lorraine Hess Hanzl, Roberta Romig, Nancy DeWalt, Jackwlyn Miles, and Elizabeth Halleman Applegate; (second row) Christine Hess Simon, Dorothy Transue, and Jacqueline Uberroth; (third row) Robert Romig, Donald Baylor, Ronald Baylor, and F. Lewis Applegate; (back row) Gerald Hottle, Edward Radcliffe, Reverend Richard Crusius, and Todd Sassaman. The Calvary church joined with St. Paul's and Zion Congregation in 1972 to form Trinity UCC.

Confirmation Class, Brith Sholom Community Center, 1953. (Gertrude Makagon.) In 1955, Rabbi Frankel wrote of Bethlehem's first Jewish residents, "All that we are and ever hope to be, we owe to those brave men and women who came to this community during the second half of the nineteenth century . . . May their courage and foresight serve as a shining example to future generations." Part of that future generation in 1953 was, from left to right: Donald H. Lipson, Vivian Weiner, Mark S. Refowich, Barbara Goodman, Allan B. Goodman, Rabbi William Frankel, Beth Neuman, Arthur Posner, Myra Ann Glazier, Alan M. Black, Deborah Makagon, and Arnold Wildfeuer.

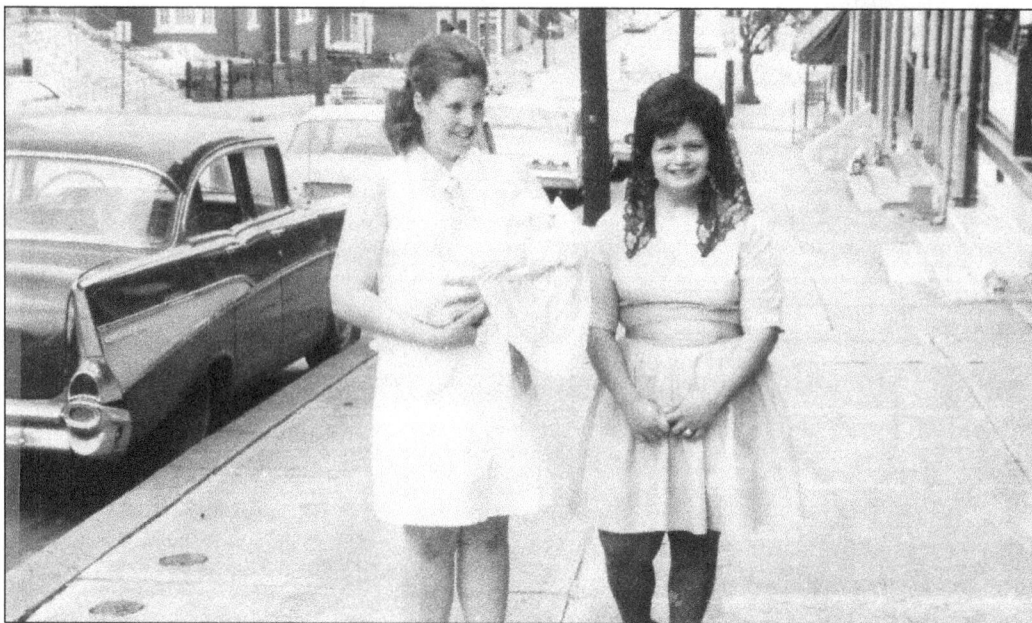

Christening Day, Rosemary Repash (mother) and Virginia Carr (godmother), East Fourth Street, 1971. (Gerald Repash.) Lifelong friends, Rosemary Repash (on the left) and Virginia Carr vowed that they would be godmothers to each other's first born child. On June 23, 1971, Virginia stood beside Rosemary as her son Gerald Repash Jr. was baptized. A 1989 graduate of Bethlehem Catholic High School, Gerald Jr. earned a bachelor's degree from East Stroudsburg University and is currently working on a master's degree in psychology from Chestnut Hill College.

Petraglia-Rosbaugh Wedding Party, Serenity Garden, 1983. (Teresa Anne Petraglia-Rosbaugh.) Theresa Petraglia and Robert Rosbaugh first met at an American Red Cross workshop while both were still in high school. They married on August 27, 1983. Theresa, a certified teacher of business education, currently works part-time for a tax consultant so she can be home after school with their son Christopher. Robert, who is from Coopersburg, spent ten years in the Navy and now works for Virginia Power and Electric. They live in Richmond, Virginia.

Six

Education

Opening day of school, Donald Essick, Ronald Belletti, Nancy Boligitz (from left to right), Northeast Middle School, 1952. (David G. Shelly.) In the early 1950s, Bethlehem's public school system began to experience the impact of the Baby Boom. A total enrollment of 10,145 students, a 527-pupil increase from the previous year, was the highest in the city since 1938. To counterbalance the increase in numbers, the new Northeast Junior High School opened its doors for the first time on September 3, 1952. Sixteen new teachers were hired that year in an effort to keep student-teacher ratios a low thirty-to-one.

Daniels School, present Edgeboro area, Esther Hahn (third from left, second row), 1904.
(Kathleen Adams.) Esther Hahn attended Daniels School, located near what is now the corner of Washington and Easton Avenues, while she was living on the outskirts of Bethlehem with her parents Thomas and Matilda and her nine siblings. Thomas, who was left nearly deaf and blind from a blast at a stone quarry where he worked, became a tenant farmer in the Edgeboro area and later in Iron Hill. Esther would ride with him on deliveries to Easton, as she would have to be his eyes and ears when crossing dangerous railroad tracks. Esther, who completed an eighth grade education, married John Hushen and during World War I worked in a local armaments factory.

Holy Infancy School (mostly Irish), first grade, Fourth and Taylor Streets, 1907. (Rose D. Hilaire.) The Holy Infancy School was established in the mid-1890s and was in the charge of the Sisters of St. Joseph. Early in its history, Holy Infancy served a mostly Irish population. Irish-Americans eventually left the area near the church at Fourth and Locust as their economic and social positions in society changed. The arrival of large numbers of Hispanics to the South Side later in the twentieth century changed the ethnic make-up of the school and church. In 1997, 265 students are enrolled at Holy Infancy School; roughly 80–90% are of Hispanic descent.

Holy Infancy School, elementary grades, Fourth and Taylor Streets, 1908. (Marie D. Scattene.) Every May, there was an annual procession in celebration of the junior sodalities of the Holy Infancy School. In 1911, over five hundred and fifty little boys and girls took part in the celebration. "The tiny ranks were in divisions, each being composed of a body of sodalities with banner bearer and aids. The girls were wreathed and bore garlands of May flowers, and the little boys wore red sashes." Without a doubt this was a special occasion for the children every year.

Rudolph's School, 1912. (Mrs. Harold Miller.) In the first decades of the twentieth century, children within the borders of Bethlehem and South Bethlehem benefitted from the establishment of both public and private schools. Between Bethlehem, West Bethlehem, and South Bethlehem, there were over a dozen public educational institutions. The continual establishment of parochial schools at area churches provided additional educational options. Yet, there were many children who lived just on the periphery, often on farms, who were unable for reasons of economy or distance to attend schools in the city. Children of many different ages would be educated in one-room schoolhouses much like Rudolph's School.

85

Graduation Day, Holy Ghost School, 1924. (Terry Draper.) Holy Ghost School was opened in September 1900. In June 1924, Cecilia Zeiner graduated from Holy Ghost at age 16. Cecilia, standing to the right of Father Fretz, was a very bright child who could write and speak Hungarian and German fluently, as well as take shorthand and type. She was the daughter of Michael, who worked at the Bethlehem Steel Company for a time and then for Bethlehem Fabricators, and Anna Zeiner. A year later, Cecilia married Joseph Betlzmann. Their wedding photograph is on page 116.

James F. Goodwin Scholarship Club, Broughal Junior High School, 1938. (Dorothy S. Johnson.) James F. Goodwin, a Bethlehem physician, established a scholarship club in 1938. Dr. Goodwin encouraged young black students to study diligently, complete high school, and go on to vocational institutions or college. He was more than an advisor and counselor to these children; he was also a friend. In 1956, a scholarship fund was established in his name to "inspire scholarship, citizenship, and a Christian way of life." Dr. Goodwin, who moved to Reading in 1940, passed away in 1982, but the memory of his desire to help young black students get a better chance in life lives on to this day.

Seventh grade class, Franklin School, Center Street, 1943. (Thomas V. Labert.) Fifty-four years later, Tom Labert still remembers most of his Franklin School classmates. From left to right are: (front row) Arlene Boyer, Stanley Rice, Nancy Lou Ayre, unidentified, Betty Hulock, Walter Siebecker, Martha Molnar, Tom Labert, unidentified, unidentified, and June Hummel; (second row) Ruth Reese, Ray Young, Louis Unangst, Herb Repsher, Nancy Barthold, Jack Ryan, Dolly Kunsman, Ray Bowers, and unidentified; (third row) unidentified, Nancy Clause, unidentified, Olga Malchuk, Robert Fenner, unidentified, unidentified, Jeanette Stocker, unidentified, and Barbara Gearhart; (back row) Mr. Cressman, Richard Cornman, John McMurtrie, unidentified, Genevieve Fisher, Dolores Auer, Gladys Long, Nevin Dunstan, and Richard Stine.

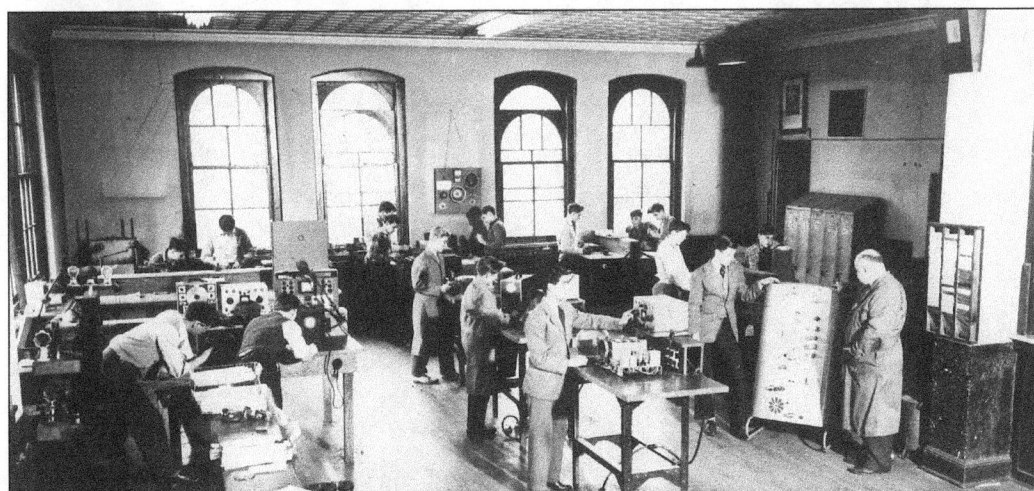

Vo-Tech Radio Shop, Old Quinn School, Fourth and Buchanan Streets, Mr. Ed Hartman, instructor, 1944. (Charles Hasenecz.) In the 1940s, the Bethlehem School District offered vocational education programs. A 1949 district publication touted the importance of technical education. "Vocational education, through proper counseling, assists the individual to choose an occupation and make intensive preparation for his life work. By its emphasis upon development of precision, safety, and manipulative skills, all groups—the youth, the veteran, and the handicapped—are offered the possibilities of obtaining greater security."

May Day, Hamilton School, Hamilton Avenue, 1934. (Ann Kennedy.) The flower girls from grade 5A were only part of the "Pretentious May Day Program at Hamilton" on May 8, 1939. As the story goes this year, Queen Elizabeth's subjects "present for her entertainment and pleasure dances, games, feats and a merry interlude of Robin Hood and Friar Tuck. Peasants appear and crown the Queen of the May and the festivities are concluded with a May Pole dance."

May Day Festival, Neisser School, sixth grade girls, Wall Street, 1950. (Thomas V. Labert.) The Neisser School celebrated May Day in 1950 with a lot of festivity as well. "Mary Anne Tretheway danced the Highland Fling as a solo number before the fourth grade pupils' rendition of the Hop Scotch polka. The traditional May Pole dance was presented by the sixth grade pupils as the climax of the program." The May Queen from the Neisser School in 1950 was Barbara Buck, who is surrounded above by her court.

Christmas Play, Ss. Simon and Jude Church School, 1956. (Ellie O'Donnell.) Ss. Simon and Jude Church was founded in July 1917. In September 1923, the church opened a parochial school to much fanfare and ceremony. Bishop McSorley said of the new school, "Let it be stated that the keystone, the arch, the superstructure . . . of the Catholic School system is the authority of God and His Blessed Son, Jesus Christ, Teacher Divine for all time." At the time of this photograph, the school was in the stages of deterioration. A new school, which accommodated over 400 students, was opened in 1967.

Second grade, Neisser School, 1955. (Mrs. John Kozero.) In 1965, twenty-one of the thirty-one second graders above graduated from Liberty High School (denoted with *). Mrs. Adams' second grade class was as follows, from left to right: (front row) Brenda Gebhart*, Barbara Grinager, Louise Myers*, John Butz*, and Elaine Shaffer; (second row) Sharon Metzgar*, Shirley Tamulavage*, Gloria Szulborski*, Bruce Hassler*, and Anita Stackhouse*; (third row) Jim Whildin*, Bob Bender*, Tom Burke*, Loretta ?, and John Nyce?; (fourth row) Jeffrey Deutch*, Roy Gruver*, Judy Phillips*, Clifford Hubbs, and Larry Steager; (back row) Mary Hawk*, Jack Ochmach?, Peter ?, Carol Abel*, Mrs. Adams, Susan Dietrich*, Francis Kozero*, Marcella Petrucella*, Stanley Van Gordon, Ricky Simons, Ricky Wagner*, and Margaret Anderson*.

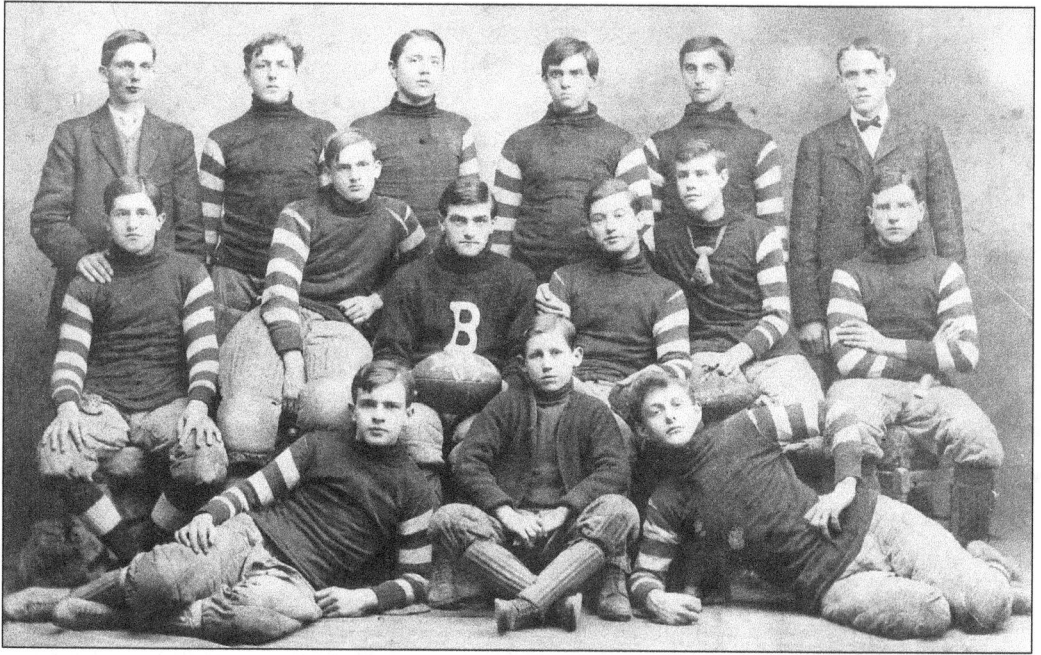

Football team, Bethlehem High School, William H. Reese Sr. (fourth from left in back row), 1907. (William H. Reese Jr.) These young men were as tough on the field as they look in this photograph. On October 19, 1907, "Bethlehem High School defeated its old time rival, Moravian Parochial School. . . .The Parochial boys put up a plucky fight, but the superior line weight and aggressiveness of the High School team was too much for them. . . . Once in the first half the Parochials carried the ball to High School's 2-yard line, where they met a stone wall of resistance that lost them the leather." After that, they did not have a chance. Bethlehem High shut out the Parochials 22-0."

Liberty High School track team in front of Liberty High, 1934. (Jean E. Scapellati.) In 1934, nearly one hundred and forty men tried out for Coach W.H. Emery's track team. Of those, he chose the strongest, fastest, and most able athletes. They were so good that the team came in second in the Penn Relays that year "by [a] margin of five inches at the tape." The Liberty High *Cauldron* said of this accomplishment, "It was here that Bethlehem upheld its reputation of constantly entering a formidable team in this event."

South Side Junior High School Champion basketball team, 1929. (Lynn Jago.) The South Bethlehem public school system was developed in the early 1870s, and the citizens believed their school system to be one of the best, "the position of its graduates in the religious, educational, industrial and commercial world, as revealed by its Alumni rolls, [being] the best proof of the excellence of the training." South Side Junior High School changed from a high school to a junior high school and back several times during this century. It is now known as Broughal Middle School.

Liberty High vs. Easton High, 1933. (Arpad Kery.) "An inspired team that struck furiously and powerfully, a well-drilled unit with all the requisites necessary for victory, brought a cherished triumph to the colors of Liberty High School Saturday afternoon on the dusty brown turf of Cottingham stadium, Easton. More than nine thousand fans, the largest crowd to see a schoolboy contest in the Valley this season, looked on with varied emotions as Liberty's inspired eleven, striking with a will at the heavier Easton array early in the game, fashioned a stirring 9 to 6 victory."

Lehigh University wrestling practice, Coach Billy Sheridan directs, 1940. (Margie Finger.) "When he came to Lehigh in the Spring of 1911, he brought more than just his exceptional talents and ability; he brought an indomitable heart, sincerity, and friendliness that were to endear him to generations of Lehigh men, and a credo of sportsmanship and fair play that was to become a heritage to all Lehigh Teams." Called "the Knute Rockne of collegiate wrestling," Billy Sheridan, a native of Loch Lemond, Scotland, arrived in the United States in January 1910, at the age 26. He began his career at Lehigh University in June 1911. In 1954, he announced his retirement from Lehigh following a career record of 223-83-7.

Junior High School Champions, Franklin Junior High football team, 1946. (David G. Shelly.) When Franklin School opened, it housed all grades, elementary through senior high. In the early twentieth century, it served as Bethlehem High until Liberty was opened in 1922. During the 1940s, population pressures, partially brought on by the influx of wartime production workers to Bethlehem and then returning GIs, transformed Franklin into a junior high school. It later was used as an elementary school until it closed in 1972. Franklin began a new life as Interim School in 1973, only to close permanently two years later, the victim of a fire. It lasted exactly 104 years, 2 months, and 24 days.

Broughal Middle School basketball team, 1978. (Junie Rich.) Coach James Rich poses with his "Number One" team and managers from Broughal Middle School after a winning 1978 season. From left to right are: (front row) Kris Rich, Joaquim Carvalho, Maria Carvalho, and Jorge Pimentel; (second row) Jack Silva, John Garcia, Raherh Perez, James Rich, Maurice Hyman, James Laska, and Mary Ann Donchez; (back row) Coach Rich, Kelvin Wilson, Jerry Matos, Clovis Williams, Alexander Coleman, and Gus Liadis.

Soccer game, Liberty vs. Dieruff, 1980. (Joseph M. Petraglia) In the first game of the season, Allentown's Dieruff High School upset Liberty's varsity soccer team, 1-0, but it was not an omen for the season. The Liberty team went on to win the District 11 soccer title that year after beating Southern Lehigh 4-1 on November 3rd. After high school, Joseph Petraglia, right, attended West Chester University, where he played soccer for four years. Joe continues to play club soccer and coach indoor and summer leagues in Bethlehem.

Seventh grade chorus, Nitschmann Junior High School, 1964. (Mary Lou Crocus.) When Nitschmann School opened on the West Side in 1922, its entire staff consisted of three teachers and included students up through the ninth grade. The school also had the district's first kindergarten. The school's population grew by leaps and bounds, however, as open fields and farmland to the west gave way to new homes. The elementary grades were moved to different schools in 1940, and a building expansion was completed in 1958.

Broughal Middle School band, 1990. (Ted Crocus.) Daniel Alonzo started as band director of Broughal Middle School in the fall of 1977. At the time, he recalls, the middle school band was one of the only bands on the South Side, and therefore they participated in many community events, including the Christmas tree lighting in Fountain Hill and the Polasky Day Parade in the spring. They also traveled outside of the area, including trips to Hershey, Boston, and Norfolk, Virginia. Daniel left Broughal in June 1993 and is now at East Hills Middle School. What he remembers most about his days at Broughal is the incredibly supportive staff and how close knit the kids in the band were.

Seven

Gatherings

Bethlehem Fairgrounds, 35 acres east of Linden Street, across from present Liberty High, 1906. (Lester B. Weiner.) The Bethlehem Fairgrounds Association was organized in 1890, and the premier opening day for the park was in June 1891. The grounds, which were widely known for the half-mile track on which Prince Alert smashed a world record in 1899, contained over 200 horse stalls. Many people would flock to the fairgrounds to enjoy the races or to just spend a day away from the city, out in the "country." The last fair was held in 1909, and the site then became a residential area.

Calypso Canoe Club Sports, Lehigh River, 1908. (Lester B. Weiner.) Every fourth of July, thousands of Bethlehemites would make their way down to Mack's Boat Landing on the Lehigh to watch the canoe races. In 1908, the festivities were nearly perfect. The "bright colors of the dresses of the ladies, the costumes of the contestants, the canoes with their flying pennants, the green of the river, etc., made a gay scene that was disturbed when intermittent showers sent spectators scurrying to sheltering trees and the canoeists to the cover of the old bridge."

Fourth of July Parade, Broad Street Bridge, 1918. (Glenn D. Koch.) Spurred by the fear of foreigners and the imperatives of World War I, nativist movements advocating "100% Americanism" grew strong in many cities during the second decade of the century . On July 4, 1918, citizens helped celebrate the most memorable Independence Day in local history, marked especially by the Loyalty Parade which lasted nearly two hours. The *Globe*'s headline read, "Cause of Freedom is Uppermost in Minds of All—Display of Patriotism is Very Evident. It was a Great Day for the Foreigner and His Showing of Absolute Loyalty Pleases. Object of Inculcating Americanization Ideas Meets With Great Success."

Float in Fourth of July Parade, The Spirit of '76, South Bethlehem, 1919. (Robert H. Daugherty.) "Bethlehem, whose community history is interwoven with the history of the republic since the days of its infancy, yesterday observed her safest and sanest Independence Day." On July 4, 1919, the people of Bethlehem gathered again to celebrate the nation's birth, but without the raucous revelry and irresponsible pyrotechnics that many in the Safe and Sane Movement had feared were ruining a once solemn occasion. This year, no accidents were reported due to drunkenness or fireworks explosions; rather, a traditional parade, water sports, and the dedicatory ceremonies of Saucon Park followed the "fitting religious program" in the morning.

Fourth of July Parade, 1925. (Tim Gilman.) Spectators lined the sides of the Hill-to-Hill Bridge for the first Fourth of July parade to pass over its new roadway. Much like celebrations of the past, early morning religious ceremonies for the city's children were followed by canoe races and water sports in the afternoon. Unfortunately, a rash of pickpocketing incidents occurred at the fireworks display held at Taylor Stadium. "Police are of the opinion that the pickpockets are of the professional class who took advantage of the vast gathering to carry out their work."

Peace Parade, Armistice Day, Broad Street Bridge, 1918. (Martha O. Luckenbach.) On November 11, 1918, all "Bethlehem was peacefully abed at 4 a.m. . . . when the first tiding of peace reached the city. Then, intermittently, the word was heralded abroad by the sounding of church bells, factory and mill sirens and whistles, by scattering auto horns and horns carried by stray celebrants; the bark of occasional revolvers and the cheers and shouts of miscellaneous men, women, and children." Later that afternoon a formal parade through the city announced the end of the Great War, and in "taking part in that celebration Bethlehem became part of the mighty upheaval of joy throughout the world."

Memorial Day Service at a burial site of Revolutionary War soldiers, First Avenue and Market Street, 1913. (Mrs. Stanley J. Heller.) "The day has come again when the deeds of heroes are recounted in every city, village, and hamlet of our land." On Memorial Day, May 30, 1913, the people of Bethlehem remembered their war heroes through parade and prayer. A parade formed at 1 pm on Main Street and wound through the town to the Revolutionary War plot, where Reverend W.H. Christ of Bethany United Evangelical congregation offered a prayer and the Bethlehem Band provided a patriotic selection.

Memorial Day Committee on Second Avenue, 1930. (Chester V. Jones.) Members of the Memorial Day Committee, headed by Elmer C. Jones, pose in front of a horse-drawn wagon. The vehicle, "conspicuous in the line of march throughout the entire day, and a familiar sight on each Memorial Day. . . conveyed the plants and flowers to the various cemeteries" and was driven by one George Heft. The two horses drawing the wagon were furnished by the Bethlehem Baking Company, seen in the rear. The other members of this committee were: (in no order) Wilbur Heft, William Wolbach, Charles G. Mack, Chaplain Christian Krier, Bertine Eschbach, Calvin Meixell, Adam Green, William Eschbach, Charles Suter, and Robert Arnold.

Memorial Day at Nisky Hill Cemetery, 1950. (Chester V. Jones.) Mayor Earl E. Schaffer told a crowd of over 1000 gathered at Nisky Hill Cemetery on May 30, 1950, "today we again are faced with uncertainties and the possibility of men making moves for world domination. We must build a nation so strong that no aggressor shall dare try to destroy the freedoms of mankind." Within a few weeks, North Korean forces crossed the 38th parallel, and the United States entered a military conflagration that would last three years.

Teddy Roosevelt on whistle stop campaign tour, Jersey Central Station, 1912. (Thomas J. Cunningham.) In April 1912, while campaigning for the Republican presidential nomination, Colonel Roosevelt of Rough Rider fame arrived at the depot of the Central Railroad of New Jersey and gave a "brief address to the assembled throng from the platform of the car of the Roosevelt Special. Admirers swarmed over the railroad, on bridges, at windows, and in treetops and telegraph poles." Having lost the nomination of the Republican Party to incumbent William Howard Taft, Roosevelt joined with other disgruntled Republicans to form the Progressive, or Bull Moose Party. Democrat Woodrow Wilson brought home victory that year, with 435 electoral votes to Roosevelt's 88 votes and Taft's 8 votes.

Harry and Bess Truman on whistle stop campaign tour, 1948. (Paul A. Pilyar.) President Harry S. Truman engaged in a rigorous whistle stop campaign across the country in 1948, stopping on October 7th at the Jersey Central Station. President Truman greeted a crowd ten thousand strong and urged them all to return a Democratic majority to the Congress when they voted in November. He assailed the "awful, do-nothing 80th Congress" and said a continued Democratic administration, House, and Senate would "assure extension of social security objectives, keep down the cost of living, and help labor and its unions to go forward."

Crowd waiting for Harry Truman's campaign train with Democratic donkey mascot, Jersey Central Station, 1948. (Anna A. Stofko.) Make that ten thousand people and one donkey who gathered to hear President Truman that day. "Spotting a real live donkey with a blanket carrying the slogan, 'We are with you Harry,' President Truman leaned out from the platform and grasped the hand of Mrs. Paul Ruyak, whose husband had provided the living symbol of the party. Mr. Ruyak was a delegate to the Philadelphia convention that nominated the Truman-Barkley ticket and rode the train from Allentown," while his wife Anna held the donkey. Nearly twelve thousand Bethlehemites cast their votes for Harry, contributing to the 24.1 million votes that lead to his upset victory over Thomas E. Dewey.

A two-family outing, Heller and Knecht families near Hellertown, 1906. (Laurenta H. Kernan.) Chances are that at a time when automobiles were not as prevalent, roads were not as smooth and tires were not as strong—an automobile outing was an event that caused much interest. A rarity, indeed, whenever a family and some friends gathered for a Sunday auto trip, the *Globe* would catch wind of it and report the fact with an entry in the "Personals" on page one.

J. Wilson Weaver family, Broadway, 1915. (Merritt F. Weaver.) "The celebration . . . is a matter of history," the *Globe* declared on October 11, 1915. "Chronicled on the bright side of the pages written by historians, will be a review of the greatest week since the incorporation of the borough." Spectacular activities and pageants, including parades, fireworks, band concerts, and "physical culture drills," were without limit during the week of October 3–9, 1915, in celebration of South Bethlehem's semi-centennial.

102

Greek "bachelors" celebrating Easter, Columbia Street, South Bethlehem, 1918. (John H. Galitis.) Proud, erect, and in a celebratory spirit, these Greek men gather for a little fraternal bonding on their day off. Greek immigrants came to Bethlehem in the first decade of the twentieth century in search of steady work and good pay that would allow them to return home with money for their families. Like most new arrivals to Bethlehem, they found work in the mills of Bethlehem Steel. Many, though, did not return home and stayed in Bethlehem, often opening up a store of their own after a time.

Porch at Locust Lodge, bungalow near Illick's Mill, 1915. (Helen Desh Woodbridge.) Locust Lodge, a log cabin along the Monocacy Creek, was the weekend retreat for Bethlehem tinsmith Maurice "Maury" Luckenbach, left. Maury, a bachelor, would invite friends (from left to right) such as Walter Rice, William Desh (owner of a butchershop on Fairview Street), and Andre Winegardner (the director of the Bethlehem Steel Company Band) to escape from city and industrial life at his retreat. The Locust Lodge was decorated with Maury's mounted prize-hunting kills, which were displayed proudly on the walls. The grounds were perfect for nature walks or pitching quoits on a Sunday afternoon.

103

Crowd waiting to enter car show at the Coliseum, 1925. (James and Marianne Anderson.) On March 21, 1925, a special sixteen-page "Automobile Edition" appeared in the *Bethlehem Globe Times* in honor of the annual Automobile Show. The *Globe* anticipated the excitement generated by the event. "The pent-up enthusiasm of motorists awaiting the annual exposition of the Lehigh Valley Automobile Show will be unleashed when the doors of the Coliseum are thrown open. . . . [The] thousands of patrons . . . can feast their eyes on the greatest collection of motor cars ever assembled under the roof of one building in this city."

Friends at the neighborhood billiard parlor, Steven Ruyak, owner, circa 1920. (Theresa M. Bartholomew.) Billiard and pool rooms were popular spots for socialization and sport in Bethlehem during the 1920s. Steven H. Ruyak's place at 431 East Fourth Street was a gathering spot for the men of the neighborhood. By 1923, Stephen had left the leisure business and was a partner at Ruyak and Bartos, an insurance and real estate company that also provided mortgage loans for people in the neighborhood. The poolroom, one of twenty-six in the city at the time, was taken over by Stephen C. Kametz.

Cremation of Calculus, Lehigh University, 1889. (Mrs. William B. Leckonby.) The Cremation of Calculus was a formal event complete with a parade through the streets of town in celebration of the sophomore class's victory over the cursed Calculus, stopping first at Moravian Seminary to address the young women. "As the Ancient Greeks, returning victorious from battle, would pay tribute to their gods, so we, in celebrating our victory over the mathematical fiend pay tribute at the shrine of the fair ones, namely the Fem. Sem. Pressing engagements with our friend Calculus prevented us during the past year from paying the proper attention to you."

Annual House Party, Sigma Phi fraternity, Lehigh University, 1959. (Arpad Kery.) Never known to be shy, retiring types, the Lehigh fraternity men of Sigma Phi in 1959 did their best to keep another university tradition alive—the Annual House Party. Under the careful supervision of Arpad Kery (standing on right) and corsage-bedecked female chaperones (in the middle), these young men from the all-male institution settled in for a little revelry with hometown sweethearts, dates from town, or young ladies from nearby women's schools, including Centenary College in New Jersey and Elmira College in New York.

New Year's Eve dance, Lehigh Temple, #930 Elks, Hotel Bethlehem, 1945. (Mrs. Dorothy Johnson.) "Bethlehem really let down its hair for one of the noisiest New Year's Eve celebrations ever recorded . . . Night clubs, hotels, and taprooms in Bethlehem were jammed to capacity as were the private clubs, social organizations and other establishments where merrymaking was a planned part of the evening's festivities." After making the rounds on December 31, 1945, the first New Year's celebration since the ending of World War II, the *Globe* "concluded with . . . certainty that there were very few quiet evenings spent last night in Bethlehem."

Individuals dressed to represent the different ethnic groups of the Lehigh Valley at Musikfest, 1989. (Margaret Barchine.) The early 1980s were gloomy years economically in Bethlehem. Merchants were closing their downtown shops, and industries were laying off hundreds of workers. Then Jeffrey A. Parks, an attorney in town, decided to do something about it. His was the brainchild that became Musikfest. Business owners, city offices, and citizen volunteers pooled their resources and put on the first Musikfest in August of 1984. A celebration of the city's and country's musical, ethnic, and historical heritage, Musikfest becomes more popular, more exciting, and more crowded every year.

Eight

Family and Friends

William H. Bodder family, 1899. (Mrs. Richard W. Jackson.) William H. and Alice Buss Bodder pose with their children at their home on Third Avenue. Born in 1848 in Lower Saucon, William worked for thirty years as a watchman at the Central Railroad of New Jersey grade crossing at Main Street. In addition, he served as treasurer of the borough of West Bethlehem prior to its annexation and aided in the construction of the Lehigh Canal. They had six children: Wilford C., Katurah, Raymond, Irene, Henrietta, and Henri.

Hesse family, Anton (father), Anton, Sara, and Otto, 1891. (Martha O. Luckenbach.) Anton F. Hess (far left) and Sara Anna Yost were married on February 13, 1860, and they had seven children. Anton, born in 1837, near Leipzig, Saxony, arrived in America in 1852. In addition to his career as a well-known bookbinder in Bethlehem, Mr. Hesse also served as School Director and as a Bethlehem Borough council member for several terms. Sara, a devout Christian and member of the Moravian church, "was of amiable disposition and was loved by all who knew her."

Wedding of M/M Joseph Horvath, studio shot, circa 1913–14. (Louis Yuhasz.) A cause for great joy, Hungarian wedding celebrations often lasted up to three days. Friends and family would gather and celebrate the union with homemade wine and traditional foods. It was probably no different for the wedding of Joseph, a steelworker originally from Hungary, and Mary Fabian Horvath. According to Louis Yuhasz, whose wife Irene (the small child in the photo) was the bride's younger sister, the wedding party would be large, and the celebrations would take place either at the local Hungarian social hall on Evans Street or in the homes of the couple's parents.

Grandpa and his girls, Samuel Henry Yost Sr., Helen Louise and Mary Elizabeth Yost, 1901. (E. Kirt and Mary Lou Muhlhausen.) Called "Grandpa" by Helen Louise and Mary Elizabeth, Samuel Yost was also "a well known venerable citizen of Bethlehem." Descendent of one of the earliest Moravian families, he arrived in Bethlehem in 1830 at age 9 and learned the trades of cigar and shoemaker. He lived on Church Street for seventy years, longer than any other resident of Bethlehem, and also ran a grocery from his residence.

Oldest living member of Central Moravian Church, Christiana Geiss Greider, age 93, 1900.
(Elizabeth M. Boyle.) Christiana Geiss Greider was born in Salisbury on September 18, 1806, and died at age 95 years, 2 months, and 12 days, making her, at the time, perhaps the oldest female member of the Moravian church. Mrs. Greider returned to Bethlehem from Louisiana following the death of her husband Henry during the Mexican War. She was a resident of the Sister's House. Christiana's great-great-great-great granddaughter, Elizabeth Boyle, is a regular at the Bethlehem Area Public Library and has done extensive research on her family with its local history collection.

An orphan boy, James Edward Gross, 1907. (Betty Gross Riter.) "Jimmy had long corkscrew blonde curls and dark blue eyes, and Laura had her heart set on the baby." Little James Edward Gross, born in 1905, was without parents before he was even two years old. His mother Emma Derr Gross died on December 29, 1906, a victim of typhoid fever. His father Weston Gross, a yardmaster for the Bethlehem Steel Company, died of injuries received in a run-away train accident at the Steel's railyards. Abe Derr, the brother of James' mother, and his wife Laura adopted the little boy following Weston's death. James graduated from Bethlehem Business College in 1924, and the following year he married Elizabeth Louise Werner, with whom he raised six children.

Bessie Jaffe Schwalb in canoe, Lehigh River, 1910. (Lillian S. Mindlin.) Bessie Jaffe's brother-in-law, Stan Steinberg, took this photograph not long before Bessie's wedding to Louis A. Schwalb in 1910. Bessie was born in Latvia and came to the United States as a young lady, settling in Hazleton, where she lived with an aunt and uncle and worked as a sewing machine operator. On a visit to her sister in Bethlehem, Bessie met and fell in love with Louis. The two were married for forty-three years, and together they operated a ladies' and gentlemen's clothing store on 3rd Street.

Moritz family, 1900. (Lila Krzanski.) The Moritz family gathered together in the yard of their home at 424 New Street in South Bethlehem for a family photograph. Matriarch Sarah, right rear, was the widow of Henry, a contractor in the city. Henry passed away in 1897, and their son George H., a carpenter and laborer for the Bethlehem Steel Corporation, remained in the family home with his mother, until his marriage. Following Sarah's death in 1905, the family home was sold.

Lawrence Beckel in automobile, Church Street, 1908. (Jane Beckel Bannan.) Born in 1851, Lawrence Levering Beckel, a lifelong member of the Moravian church and a well-known local machinist, was educated at the Moravian Parochial School and Lehigh University. A bridge builder and a night foreman for the No. 2 machine shop at the Steel, Mr. Beckel opened an automobile repair shop and garage on South Main Street. He and his wife Elizabeth Barett Hooven Beckel had two children and resided at 351 Church Street. He relocated his shop to his residence and continued his repair business there until his death in 1909.

William Pike's 34-inch eel caught in the Monocacy Creek, at age 100, 1925. (Nancy Zulli.) William Pike, originally from Cornwall, England, arrived in the United States in 1881 and worked in Philadelphia for the Philadelphia Hosiery Company. Also an umbrella-maker, he taught the trade to his son Charles. William often came to Bethlehem to examine operations of this city's plant and to visit Charles. At the time of his death in 1931, William was rumored to be the oldest living man in the country.

Boxers, Harry Jr. and Robert Stofflet, 318 West Third Street, 1915. (Tina Juckett.) In 1901, Harry Stofflet, a worker at the Bethlehem Iron Company, married Barbara Maurer, who had come to the United States from Germany at age 3 in 1881. While Harry worked in the Bessemer office, Barbara stayed home to care for her two sons, Harry Jr. and Robert. Their daughter Catherine was born in April of the same year this photograph was taken. Though he never became a prize pugilist, Robert, now 91, did lead a life of interesting adventure as an airplane pilot, the captain of several private yachts, and as an avid hunter.

Robert W. Hunsicker, seventh birthday, 1924. (Mrs. Robert W. Hunsicker.) Robert W. was born in 1918 to Robert and Elizabeth Hunsicker, who had met when both were employed by the Schwab family. Robert Sr. was Mr. Schwab's chauffeur, and Elizabeth was Mrs. Schwab's traveling companion. Robert Sr. died in 1918 during the influenza epidemic. Following this tragedy, Robert W. and his mother stayed with the Schwab family until he was two years old. He then lived in Bethlehem with his grandmother while his mother served as nanny to William Randolph Hearst's grandchildren in New York City. Robert wed Pauline Bealer on May 25, 1940, and over the years worked for Western Electric, Air Products, and Bethlehem Steel, from which he retired.

Friends, Theresa Csrenko Petrusic and Anna Holecz Piskula (seated from left to right), and unidentified and Frances Holecz Dodig (standing on the right), Central Park, Rittersville, 1916. (Marie Trilli.) Not only could four friends on an outing to Central Park, "Where Nature Has Bestowed Her Choicest Gifts," get their picture taken, but they could also enjoy the shooting galleries, the carousel, the Giant Derby Racer, and the lavish picnic areas of "Pennsylvania's Greatest Pleasure Ground." Operating from Memorial Day through early September, Central Park drew flocks of people not only to its amusements, but also to free band concerts and comedic play performances.

"Their Best Behavior": Lorraine (on left) and Arlene Druckenmiller, Goepp Street, 1928. (Arlene V. Wesner.) O.O. Druckenmiller, originally from Treichlers, wed Bethlehem native Clara Kemmerer in the early 1920s. They soon had two beautiful daughters, Arlene and Lorraine, with four more children to follow over the next twenty years. Lorraine, 70, and her husband Stephen Kubat had nine children and have lived on the West Coast for forty-five years. Arlene, now 72, has been married to Kenneth Wesner for fifty-three years. They raised four children.

Confirmation portrait, Miss Mary Kepp, studio shot, 1918. (Carl Robert Nicholls.) Edward Kepp, a laborer at the Steel, and Savannah Hawk had a daughter Mary in 1903. Mary grew up in the boarding house on Fourth Street owned by Edward's mother and run by Savannah, who made it her mission to feed adults and children alike when she found them scrounging for food during the Depression. Mary wed Robert Nicholls and gave birth to a son, Carl Robert, in 1938. Before Carl reached age 5, his father was seriously injured in an accident at the Steel and died soon thereafter. Mary went to work at Hellertown Manufacturing after her husband's death and with Savannah's help raised Carl, who still lives in Bethlehem.

Posing near George Washington profile rock formation, Crissie E. Hake and Mr. and Mrs. Ralph Bell, 1912. (Mary A. Swartz.) Earlier in the century, when the work week was six days and sometimes over sixty hours long, Sunday was often the only day of leisure for people in industrial areas like Bethlehem. Dr. Richmond Myers pointed out that "On Sunday afternoon walks it was the custom to retain much of the finery worn to church in the morning with possible slight modifications of comfort. . . . One practical reason . . . was that often the Sabbath walk ended with an informal call" on an acquaintance or two back in town.

Wedding of Joseph and Cecilia Beltzmann, studio shot, 1925. (Terry Draper.) Joseph A. Beltzmann wed Cecilia Zeiner on July 15, 1925. Joseph had been born in Germany on June 25, 1905. His father Joseph Sr. is seated next to him. His mother Mary was living in Germany and was unable to attend the wedding. Cecilia's father Michael also attended his daughter alone, for his wife Anna had already passed away. Regardless, the couple celebrated their special day with many close relatives. They set up house at 626 Bradley Street and raised three children, Joseph R., Cecilia, and Theresa. Joseph A. retired from the Bethlehem Steel Corporation in 1965, after thirty-five years in the HDM forge specialty shop.

116

Michalerya family—John, Mary, Maria, Peter, Charles, and Michael (from left to right), 1925. (Charles Michalerya.) A strong, robust man, Charles Michalerya immigrated to the United States in 1910 from a small Russian Orthodox village in Austria-Hungary and went to work in the rolling mills of Bethlehem Steel. Many immigrants from the same village or nearby area settled on the South Side as well and became part of the Michalerya's extended family. Charles and his wife, Mary, had a total of eight children. All of Charles' sons followed him into the steel mills, except his youngest, Charles Jr., who worked for thirty years at Hellertown Manufacturing, makers of Champion Spark Plugs.

Taylor-Martin family, 1934. (Barbara Martin Stout.) A family of influence and civic consciousness, the Taylor-Martin clan took a breather from business and community outreach to pose for a family photograph. Patriarch Robert Sayre Taylor (center), a prominent Bethlehem attorney for over fifty years, was a member of St. Luke's Board of Directors for twenty-six years and was a charter member of the Bethlehem Community Chest. Robert and his wife Caroline had a son and daughter, Robert Jr. (right) and Frances (left). Robert Jr. followed in both his father's professional and civic footsteps. Frances married Edmund F. Martin, who began at the Steel in 1922 and became chairman and chief executive officer.

Grandmother Mariana Lopez holding Edward with Velia, Manuel, and Gilbert (from left to right), 1934. (Edward J. Lopez.) Mariana Lopez and her husband operated a small grocery store in Hellertown near the Coke Works, where so many Mexican immigrants found work in the 1920s–1930s. Knowing the transition to the rigors of life at the Steel was difficult and unpredictable, they always extended credit to their fellow countrymen when needed. Mariana encouraged her four grandchildren to work hard, learn English, and become good citizens; they did. Manuel A., like his father, worked for the Steel, but as a draftsman. Velia was for many years a bookkeeper for the *Bethlehem Globe Times*. Gilbert J. served as Assistant Principal at Liberty High School and eventually retired as Principal of Marvine Elementary School. Edward, the youngest of the four, also worked for a time at the *Globe* and won $5.7 million in the lottery in 1985. He now owns Classic Realty in Bethlehem. Mariana would be proud.

Home at the Labor Camp, Manuel Lopez Sr. and sons Edward and Gilbert, South Bethlehem, 1934. (Velia M. Dugan.) Lured by promises of steady work and steady pay, hundreds of Mexican men and their families flocked to Bethlehem in the 1920s. Manuel Lopez and his wife Mary arrived in Bethlehem in 1926. The Lopez family set up home at the company-sponsored Labor Camp, where Mary took care of their four children while Manuel worked as a coal handler at the works. They remained at the Labor Camp in their one-floor frame building until around 1940, when they moved to Princeton Avenue.

Mexican families and friends — Campos, Ramos, Duran, Lazaro, and others, 1937. (Maria V. Ruiz.) The Bethlehem Steel Corporation sponsored the trains that met anxious Mexican immigrants at the Texas border and brought them north to Bethlehem to work in the coke ovens. The trip was not free, as the fares for the train ride were deducted from their salaries. They dubbed the community they established at the camp "Little Mexico." Like most immigrants to industrial America, the Mexicans formed close ties with other new arrivals from home, which made their adjustment to this country easier, less traumatic, and often very successful.

Charles Michalerya, age 6, East Seventh Street, South Bethlehem, 1938. (Charles Michalerya.) According to Charles Michalerya, just about every kid on the South Side had his picture taken by the traveling photographer who owned this pony. The dimes earned by selling scrap to the local junk dealer gained the boys access to the Western movies showing at any one of the South Side's four theaters: the Globe, the Palace, the College, or the Lehigh. Fantasies inspired by these matinees were briefly fulfilled when the photographer dressed the children in hats, bandanas, and chaps over their street clothes, and sat them atop this little Shetland pony, who clearly loved the job!

Sidewalk cowboy, James G. Whildin Jr., 1953. (James G. Whildin Jr.) In 1950s Bethlehem and all across the country, there were always willing youngsters hungry for a rousing game of "Cowboys and Indians." Hopalong Cassidy, above, had no trouble rounding up other cowboys in the neighborhood for shootouts and rides into the sunset. Born in 1947 in Durham, North Carolina, James Whildin Jr. moved to Bethlehem with his parents James Sr. and Marjorie after his father's graduation from Duke Medical School. This photograph was taken outside Dr. Whildin's radiology office at 134 East Broad Street, where the family also lived. James Jr. graduated from Liberty High School in 1965. After receiving degrees from Duke University and the University of Pennsylvania, James Jr. returned to Bethlehem. An architect for Spillman Farmer, he lives here with his wife, AnneMarie Linkert Whildin, and their children, Emily and Chris.

"My Sweetheart": Glenn R. Lee and Nancy A. Johnson, 1952. (Mrs. Catharine Lee.) Glenn R. Lee and Nancy A. Johnson were engaged on Valentine's Day in 1952. While sitting in the Boyd Theatre watching a newsreel of Elizabeth II's ascension to the throne of England, Glenn popped the question and gave Nancy her engagement ring on the spot. Glenn spent a brief time at home following basic training and soon after this photograph was taken, headed for Loring Air Force Base in Maine. Following his time in the service, Glenn received his degree from Kutztown University and went on to teach at Hiram W. Dodd School in Allentown for thirty-one years. He and Nancy celebrated their forty-third anniversary on April 24, 1997.

Robert H. Stewart family, 1951. (Robert H. Stewart.) Robert, a metallurgical observer for the Bethlehem Steel Corporation for forty-four years, and his wife Mary, a homemaker, married on May 27, 1944. Together they raised their three daughters, Bonnie, Holley (baby), and Barbara (sitting in Robert's lap) in this house on Easton Avenue, where they still live. All three little girls grew to be successful women. Bonnie, an LPN, and her husband raised three daughters and now live in Schenectady, New York. Holley, a graduate of Moravian College, is a chemist and lives in Michigan with her husband, a Moravian minister. Barbara, the mother of two, is married to a former editor of the *Bethlehem Globe Times*. They reside in Pittsburgh.

Ready to ride, 1940. (Mr. Joseph F. Horwath.) The Horwath family performs the great American ritual: posing in front of the new car. And what a car! The Dodge Deluxe Series included "Air Foam seat cushions, dual electric windshield wipers, chrome beltline trim moldings, a deluxe steering wheel with hornring, chrome moldings in the lower bodysides, and rich upholstery." With over eighty thousand produced, this four-door sedan was Dodge's most popular model and sold for just over $900.00.

Stephen Kozo and children, Stephanie and Ronald, 1946. (Sheila and Tony Kozo.) Scarcity of consumer goods during the war meant people had no choice but to save their money or invest in government bonds. After World War II, many young families were able to purchase new cars and homes with money they earned either as GIs or from working overtime for wartime production. Stephen Kozo and his children, Stephanie and Ronald, pose in front of their new 1946 Chevy. Stephen worked as a welder at Bethlehem Steel while his wife, Theresa, stayed home with their five children, Ronald, Stephanie, Anthony, Priscilla, and Annette.

Bob Miller and sons, 12th Avenue, 1950. (Jon Kidd Miller.) Robert Miller takes his sons Robin and Jon for a ride around the backyard on one of the miniature railroads from his own Miller Backyard Railroad Mfg. Co. He sold over one thousand kits between 1950 and 1960. Not only a railroad enthusiast, Robert, an Army Air Corps veteran of World War II, served on the city council from 1962 to 1966 and was a chairman of the Bethlehem Public Library Board. He was instrumental in the fund-raising for the public library building at 11 West Church Street and in the construction of the city center across the plaza.

Commander—Slovak Gymnastic Union, Sokol Lodge #93, Victor Karabin and Joseph Karabin Sr., 1965. (Joseph B. Raykos) Joseph Karabin (right), a schedule clerk at the Steel for forty-two years, carried on the family and ethnic tradition of active membership in the National Sokol Lodge of South Bethlehem. For many of Slovak heritage, associational life in Sokol is a family affair where lifelong relationships are established, especially at gymnastic meets between different Sokol organizations. Joseph's son Victor turned his love for physical fitness into his lifework as a health and physical education professor. Joseph's daughter Teena Karabin Coleman and granddaughter Christine are still active in Sokol, as a family tradition continues on.

Rakos-Raykos family reunion, National Sokols Club, South Bethlehem, 1968. (Barbara A. Raykos.) Twenty-four-year-old Stephen Rakos arrived in Bethlehem in 1912 with several buddies from his hometown in Czechoslovakia. A year later, he met and married his wife Anna, also from Czechoslovakia. He worked in the blast furnace of the Steel for forty-three years, and Anna worked in the local silk mills. Together, they raised twelve children. Five of six sons followed their father into the mills, including one son, Joseph, who worked there for over forty years as a carpenter. Combined, this family has dedicated over 180 years of service to the Steel.

Wedding anniversary, Mr. and Mrs. Charles H. Pike, 1946. (Nancy Zulli.) Charles, the son of William Pike, was born in County Cork, Ireland. He and his wife Ruth married in 1896, and Charles set up his umbrella business in Bethlehem. Pictured above is their family who helped them celebrate their fifty years together. From left to right are: (front row) great-granddaughter Nancy Unkle Zulli, Charles and Ruth Pike, Betty Nagle Hoerner, and Wilbur Pike; (back row) Grace Pike, Charles Nagle, Stella Nagle, Marion Nagle Unkle, and James Asher Unkle.

Laufer's Hardware Store staff, 219–225 Broadway, 1984. (Irene E. Horvath.) Laufer's Hardware, originally located at 411 Wyandotte Street, is Bethlehem's oldest hardware store, having been established by Milton Laufer in 1876. John Horvath (on the left) went to work at Laufer's in 1947. Soon after he and his wife Irene were married in 1954, they took over as proprietors of the business. The store was a family affair, employing their daughters Mary Ann and Dyanne and son John Jr. for a time. The Horvath's sold the store in 1989, but a nephew, Bruce Horvath, presently runs it with his partner Andrew Lukievics.

126

Little patriot, Memorial Day Parade, Linden Street, 1990. (Leslie Kilbourne Druschel.) Just three years old in 1990, little Gayden Druschel was already learning about pride of country and respect for the veterans who have fought our wars. While Gayden may have been mostly interested in waving a small American flag in time with the American Legion Band, U.S. District Judge Franklin Van Antwerpen reminded the crowd of the heroism of our veterans. "They answered the call. They did what had to be done. They were there when we needed them." While it is important to remember and reminisce about the people and the places of the past, Bethlehemites continually strive to preserve and improve their community for the future of every little patriot.

Notes on Sources

Any historical work that incorporates original research should include acknowledgment of all primary resources. Since the photos selected from the 250th Anniversary display are the focus of this work, it seemed inappropriate to waste valuable layout space on a bibliography and endnotes. However, we believe we have come to a compromise that abides by the standards of scholarly etiquette, while retaining the integrity of the exhibit photos within this work.

A bibliography and notes on every photograph used in *Bethlehem* is on file at the Bethlehem Area Public Library at 11 West Church Street in Bethlehem for perusal by anyone interested. Whether it is out of curiosity, for the purpose of learning more about the events depicted, or just to double check the work, all interested parties are encouraged to stop by the library and make use of these references.

This is the appropriate space, as well, in which to make special note of perhaps the most valuable resources incorporated in the research for this work: the personal recollections provided by those who took the time and energy to donate photos to both the exhibit and this book. Their memories of family and place surely enriched this work beyond all expectation. Though they are too numerous to mention here, their contributions do not go unnoticed or unappreciated, and they, as well, are acknowledged in the reference notes.

www.ingramcontent.com/pod-product-compliance
Lightning Source LLC
Chambersburg PA
CBHW080849100426
42812CB00007B/1974